Tempus
Two in One Series

AROUND
TRING

Tring decorated in honour of Prince of Wales visit to Halton Jan'y 15th to 18th 1884

In 1884, Mr Alfred de Rothschild entertained the Prince of Wales at his mansion at Halton, which had only been completed the previous year, having been started around three years earlier. The Prince came by special train from Euston and Mr Rothschild drove his carriage to Tring station to meet him. Although it was only a private visit, the people of Tring decorated the town, knowing that he would drive through at the beginning and end of his stay. A grand ball was arranged by Mr Rothschild and his mansion and grounds were illuminated by electric lighting, including arc lights from the towers. This astonished onlookers since electric light had only been invented a few years before.

Tempus
Two in One Series

AROUND
TRING

Compiled by
Mike Bass and Jill Fowler

TEMPUS

This edition first published 2001
Copyright © Mike Bass and Jill Fowler, 2001

Tempus Publishing Limited
The Mill, Brimscombe Port,
Stroud, Gloucestershire, GL5 2QG

ISBN 0 7524 2211 1

Typesetting and origination by
Tempus Publishing Limited
Printed in Great Britain by
Midway Clark Printing, Wiltshire

Originally produced as two books:

Around Tring
First published 1996
Copyright © Mike Bass and Jill Fowler, 1996
ISBN 0 7524 0371 0

Around Tring: The Second Selection
First published 1998
Copyright © Mike Bass and Jill Fowler, 1998
ISBN 0 7524 1004 0

IMAGES
of England

AROUND
TRING

Compiled by
Mike Bass and Jill Fowler

TEMPUS

Gilbert Grace & Son in Western Road, later renamed the High Street. In the 1880s it had been further down, at 34 High Street, before that in Akeman Street, and in the 1870s Sebastian Grace had promises near the old Market House, demolished in 1900, that stood in the front of the church. It was established in 1750, possibly in Frogmore Street. Graces were the manufacturers of many of the beautiful wrought iron gates seen in the early photographs. They also did a lot of work for the Rothschilds in the construction of the Museum, and are still a successful traditional ironmongers. Mrs Emma Grace, the great-grandmother of the present Gilbert Grace, can be seen in this photograph.

Contents

Acknowledgements

Wendy Austin: Hugh and Margaret Bass: Jean Bradding: Bert Brooks
Connie Carter: Cholesbury-cum-St Leonards History Society
George Christopher: George Cobby: John and Pam Cockerill: Peter Cook
Mick Higgins: Shirley Fisher: Frank Gower: Pat Gower
Peter and Thelma Gower: Bob Grace: Gilbert and Julie Grace: Nora Grace
Phil and Gary Harrop: Jeff Hawkins: Stephen Hearn
Hedley and Dulcie Hopcroft: the late Bob Hummer: Audrey Kempster
David Kempster: Ron Kitchener: Florence and Gordon McAndrew
Pat Moss-Carlsson: Doreen Moy: Mrs Nurden: George and Dorothy Prentice
Arthur Reed: Don and Ann Reed: Janet and Simon Rigby: John Rotheroe
Ralph Seymour: Doug Sinclair: Peggy Slemeck: Jeannie and Frank Standen
Mrs Roland Stevens: Eirlys Thomas
Tring and District Local History and Museum Society: 1st Tring Scout Group
Tring Park Cricket Club: Philip Watts: Ron Wheeler.

Introduction

Tring is first mentioned in the Anglo-Saxon Record of AD 571, several centuries before nearby larger towns. In the Domesday book, compiled in 1086 on the instruction of William the Conqueror, it was called Treunge or Tredunga. By the thirteenth century one of the names referring to the town was Trehanger, a name given to a ladies social club in Tring seven centuries later. The town's position where the ancient Icknield Way crossed the Roman road, Akeman Street, ensured opportunities for local merchants to trade, and, with the coming of the Grand Junction Canal and the London to Birmingham Railway Company early in the nineteenth century, Tring soon became a prosperous and thriving market town.

Tring is said to have had a parish church for more than 700 years, but little, if anything, is left of the first building on the site, which probably predates the Norman Conquest. Some of the interesting features in the church date back to the fifteenth century, such as the original arches and the stone corbels between them, but there have been a lot of alterations and rebuilding since then. The church contains six bells, dating from 1624 to 1882, when a major restoration was completed. Other denominations are also well represented in Tring and in the surrounding villages most of the churches date in part back to the twelfth or thirteenth century, an exception being St Cross, Wilstone, completed in 1877.

The arrival of Nathaniel Rothschild, of the famous banking family, to Tring Park in 1872 made a considerable impact on the people of Tring. He and Lady Rothschild took a benevolent interest in the town and employed local people in the various projects in which they were involved. It was said that if an unemployed local person approached Lord Rothschild's agent he would be found a position somewhere on the estate. Nathan's son, Walter, founded the Tring Museum which was opened to the public in 1892. Today the magnificent displays of birds, animals and insects are part of the British Museum and attract thousands of visitors a year.

A lot of older buildings in Tring have disappeared, due in the early days to the Rothschilds' clearance for their own projects, and due later to council redevelopment. However much remains that can still be recognised when compared with Victorian and Edwardian photographs, and descendants of many of the old families still live in Tring. The town is still a pleasant place in which to live, there are no multi-story car parks, no green glass skyscrapers and no giant supermarkets, though an application for one of the latter has been put forward recently. The Tring by-pass, opened in 1975, has relieved the traffic congestion in the centre of the town to some extent, but parking is still a problem, especially in the older parts where the houses were built some time before the invention of the motor car.

We have tried to gather together a collection of photographs that reflects the character of Tring and shows how the people lived, worked and enjoyed themselves. The descriptions of the photographs have been written with the help of many of the older citizens of the town, often remembering people and events dating back over fifty years. We thank them all and hope we have recorded the facts correctly. If you feel you can add anything more to the story of Tring in the past we would be very pleased to hear from you.

One
Around the Town

Western Road, Tring.

Western Road in around 1914 viewed from the Chapel Street–Miswell Lane crossroads. The Anchor public house is much the same today, as are the cottages beyond it. Mr Rolfe's house and the Western Hall in the centre of the photograph have now been demolished to make way for the new houses in Stanley Gardens.

Two photographs taken early this century of Western Road. Above, between the two blocks of houses (see page 37) was Mr Hobbs stonemasons yard. Next to the last block is now a more modern detached house and next to that used to be the Regal Cinema, built in 1936. The Regal was demolished in 1960 and ten flats built on the site, named Regal Court. The view below has changed little.

The Upper High Street in the 1880s, then called Western Road. After Prouse's, the saddlers, can be seen the Post Office but beyond that more shops have yet to be built. On the right is Ivy Cottage, Miss Wilson's Dame School, and beyond that can be seen the National School.

Tring High Street *c.* 1910. A Whitsun procession has paraded through the town and is returning to the school before going to the Park for a picnic. These processions continued until well into the century.

Tring High Street *c.* 1904 at the Frogmore Street–Akeman Street crossroads. The Market House is on the right but the police station has yet to be built next to it. Mr William Bayman Humphrey of Park Road stands at the front. He looks a dignified gentleman and for many years represented the Imperial Fire Insurance Company. A retired builder, Mr Humphrey died on 21 May 1920 and was buried on his ninety-fourth birthday.

The corner of Akeman Street and the High Street in the 1890s, from the crossroads upwards. The house is that of Mr Mead, the butcher, and beyond is his shop and slaughterhouse. The buildings stood well out into the street and made the main road very narrow at this point. In the distance the National School building can just be seen.

Market House, Tring

The Market House on the corner of Akeman Street. It was built at the turn of the century on the site of Mr Mead's premises, replacing the old Market House in front of the church. It was opened in 1901, designed by Lord Rothschild's architect, William Huckvale, and paid for by local subscription as a memorial to Queen Victoria's Diamond Jubilee.

The Market House in the 1970s, the ground floor was enclosed around 1910. It was later used to house the fire engine and the fire siren was in the bell tower on the roof. The larger size of modern fire engines necessitated the move to a purpose-built fire station in Brook Street. The police station can be seen just beyond the Market House.

The High Street in the 1930s. On the left is Arthur Gates, stationers, now The Motorists Centre. In the distance De Fraines, also a stationers, was on the corner just this side of the Rose and Crown Hotel. The imposing building with the pillars is the Nat West Bank, which is this side of the Midland Bank. Adjacent to it are the premises that housed the doctor's surgery until a purpose-built surgery was recently opened in Western Road. Lovibonds, the wine merchant, was still trading well within living memory, and Smith's Chemist remains, renamed Lloyds.

The High Street in the 1890s. In the far distance the public house, The Green Man can just be seen. This side of it the tall ivy-covered building is the premises of Ebenezer Charles Bird, booksellers, stationers and printers. It was later demolished by the Rothschilds and replaced by the mock-Tudor house built for their estate accountant. At this time the old Rose and Crown was level with the other shops which have been rebuilt early this century. On the left we see the premises of Brown & Foulkes, now Brown & Merry estate agents, but the shops and old Market House beyond were part of the clearance to open up the view to the church.

14

Tring High Street *c.* 1900. John Bly Senior opened his shop at 22 High Street in the early 1890s, selling china and furniture, the forerunner of the well known antique business. They later moved to 50 High Street, and the Midland Bank was built on the site of this and the butchers shop next door. On the left one of Tring's oldest inns, The Bell can just be seen.

The High Street around 1960 after Sanders, the fruiterers, had closed. Clements the jewellers, watch and clockmakers, was still open. Both were demolished to make the entrance to the Dolphin Square shopping precinct.

Tring High Street in the early 1880s. This scene depicts a parade of the Society of Oddfellows and the Tring Band surrounded by locals. Butchers Bank, now the Nat-West is on the left, and in the far distance is Ivy Cottage. At this time there were few other buildings on that part of the High Street.

The High Street in the 1880s, with Butchers Bank on the left. Just beyond, Mr William Johnson stands outside his butchers shop where he lived with his wife Sarah, their two sons and four daughters. Next door Mr Henry Johnson kept the fishmongers shop, and the large arch past the surgery is the entrance to Tring Brewery, occupied by John Brown. On the right is the Bell Inn and Sharman's clothes shop.

16

The High Street in 1900, as the old Market House was being knocked down. It was demolished because the people of Tring wanted to build a new Market House to commemorate Queen Victoria's Diamond Jubilee. Old records tell of a Market House in 1650 with a corn loft over it. A description of 1819 said it was 'a mean edifice on wooden pillars having a pillory and cage underneath'. Any person found wandering the streets of Tring who was the worse for drink could end up spending the night locked in the cage. The area up to the Brown & Merry building was cleared and was left open so all could enjoy the view of the church.

Tring High Street in the 1970s. The view of the church as it has been seen from the Rose and Crown forecourt after both the old Market House and Rose and Crown had been demolished. It remained a car park until the High Street improvements in 1991, which then gave an even better view of the church.

The Lower High Street on market day in the 1890s. The Rothschilds moved the livestock market from this High Street site, where it had been held for many centuries, down to a new purpose-built market in Brook Street. The general market stayed on this roadside location until the 1970s.

Market day in the 1970s. As in the previous picture the market is still on the pavement in the Lower High Street. When the new car park was built on the grassed area behind these stalls, the Friday market was held there as it is today.

The far end of the High Street with Station Road in the distance. The decorations are for the visit of the Prince of Wales, later King Edward VII, in 1897, the year of Queen Victoria's Diamond Jubilee. Mr Woodman stands outside his Green Man Inn.

The London Road, Brook Street end of Tring with another procession, in the thirties, turning to march back through the town. The Unity Hall is on the left, and on the hill can be seen the rectory, later demolished, and now there are modern houses on the site.

Tring Market, Brook Street. The Market was built by the Rothschilds in the 1880s. There had been a livestock market in Tring since the thirteenth century but before it moved to Brook Street it would have been held in the High Street, called 'Market Street'. The business was run for many years by Messrs W. Brown & Co, and more recently by Brown & Merry, the estate agents and auctioneers. Although it retains the name, it is now owned by Mr Stephen Hearn. The livestock sales have been phased out and now the buildings are the venue for general goods and fine art sales.

Christchurch Road in the 1960s when it was still a No Through Road. In the distance can be seen Osmington School, formerly Okeford House, and the road did not go far beyond that point. The detached houses were just being built along each side of the road, and the entrance to Goldfield Road is on the left.

Henry Street. The small streets of Tring were seldom photographed unless an interesting event was taking place, as here, on Jubilee Day in May 1935. The couple at the front are Emily and Alfred Crockett who lived at No. 30. Mr Crockett had been a carrier all his working life and is remembered driving the railway horse and cart. In the 1891 census Emily and Alfred were living at No. 30, and were aged twenty-two and twenty-four respectively. The tall figure standing in the road on the left is Jack Smith.

Looking up Chapel Street in the 1960s. The cottages remain mostly unchanged but the barn and the corner premises, formerly a builders yard owned by the Finchers and later by Potter Bros. plumbers and decorators, have been replaced by the new doctors surgery. In the distance can be seen St Marthas church and the large tree that became a victim of the gales some years later.

King Street in the 1970s, with the Kings Arms in the distance. Behind the trees was the big house, The Furlong, built by the Revd Arthur Frederick Pope in the middle of the last century. More recently it was used as the Convents Junior School but was demolished in the late 1980s and replaced by flats and gardens, also called The Furlong. This part of King Street was built on land known as Gravelly Furlong and the house just visible beyond the trees is now called Gravelly House.

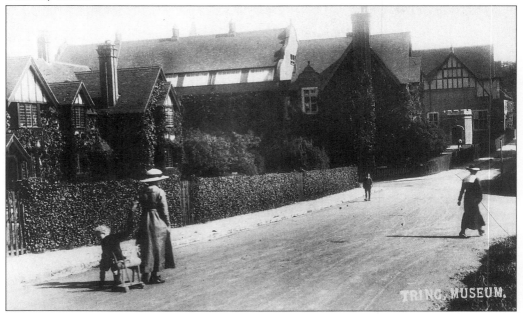

Park Road early this century, showing the Museum, in the background, and the Louisa Cottages on the left. The turning to the left is Akeman Street, ahead is Park Street and to the right is the Chesham Road. These buildings are still much the same today.

Looking down Akeman Street, from Park Road, in the 1870s. The men on the left are in front of The Swan public house while the lady in the crinoline is standing by the premises of Mr Evans the silk weaver, later Rodwell's brewery. In the distance is the Royal Oak, one of five public houses in Akeman Street. On the right, where the Rothschild Museum will soon be built, is the barn of Mr Fincher's Town Farm.

Closed shops and cottages on the Akeman Street–Albert Street corner just before they were demolished to make way for the new buildings of the William Batey electronics business, already in Akeman Street. In 1882 the corner building was occupied by Joseph Budd, a 'Marine Store Dealer' and later, in 1910, Ebenezer Prentice was running the business.

Akeman Street contains some of the oldest buildings in Tring. On the right is Graces Mill, now called Graces Maltings and parts of this building go back to medieval times. Opposite the Mill was a bakers run by Edward Grace and his wife Jane which later became Warriors bakery shop. Further down is the Harrow public house which was pulled down in the late 1950s. The area behind is still called Harrow Yard. The building at the end of the street is Mr Mead's house which was knocked down when the Market House was built.

Cato's weaving shop in Park Road in the 1890s. There were several weaving shops in Tring, making rough canvas for items like horses nosebags through to fine canvas used for embroidery. Cato's started originally in Tabernacle Yard in Akeman Street but George Cato later ran his business at 12 Charles Street. The premises in Park Road employed a lot of young boys who were 'half-timers' from school. The building was later demolished as part of Lord Rothschild's clearance of the south side of Park Road. The Chapel Street–King Street junction can just be seen in the distance.

An early photograph of Parsonage Place. In the 1890s James Darvill and his wife Rachel lived in Parsonage Place Farm with their four nephews and nieces. Although this area has been altered over the years, many of the buildings still exist as modernised private dwellings.

A view of Parsonage Place in the 1970s. The large ancient barn at the back has sadly been severely damaged after a nearby shed was set alight and the fire spread to the barn. The building just this side of it can be seen on the left-hand side of the photograph above. In the 1890s some eight families lived in Parsonage Place including shoe makers, plumbers and decorators, straw plaiters and carpenters. The cottages have now been renovated and are again occupied.

Frogmore Street photographed in 1971. In the 1890s Johnson's fish shop was still a private house and part of Frogmore Street. Hy Johnson, fishmonger, first appears in Kellys Directory in 1899. It is now No. 1 Parsonage Place, and has been a restaurant for some years. In the far distance is Barnetts the bakers which, in the 1880s, was run by Ann Putman, and in the 1930s by Edwin Burch. Many of the buildings on the right have now been demolished and replaced by the Dolphin Square shopping centre. The Dolphin Inn used to stand in the space between the buildings on the right in this photograph

Frogmore Street photographed in the early 1970s. The building on the far right is Barnetts the bakers. The low building next to it still stands but the other two have since been demolished. In 1891 the central building was the premises of Alfred Chapman, pawnbroker, and to the left lived the Revd Charles Pearce, Baptist minister. This is now the entrance to the Frogmore Street car park.

New Mill in the 1930s. Brook Street stretches into the distance on its way to Tring. The public house on the left is The Pheasant, now refurbished and renamed The New Mill.

Wingrave Road c. 1930. Benjamin Saunders Gower ran the post office and store, seen on the right, which is now a hairdressers. The other cottages have changed little, although The Queens Arms, in the distance, has gone.

Grove Road, leading to New Mill. Marshcroft Lane leads off to the right.

Grove Road, Tring.

Houses in Grove Road, in the 1950s which look much the same today.

A row of houses in Marshcroft Lane, off Grove Road, leading to Park Hill Farm.

A closer view of the last pair of houses, showing the handsome windows and tile-hung walls of these Pendley Estate houses.

Plans for the Grand Junction Canal were drawn up in 1791, the chief engineer being William Jessop. Work was started in 1793 and since all the work was done by hand, it took 6,000 people around four years to complete it, at the cost of about a million pounds. The canal, now called the Grand Union, saw considerable trade for almost two centuries, the last regular commercial traffic being in the 1980s. Pleasure boats and fisherman are still a regular feature of the canal and the miles of towpaths attract walkers.

Goldfield Mill at the top of Miswell Lane. The mill was built in 1840 by Mr Grover, formerly in partnership with the Mead family, who had their business at New Mill. Mr Grover had a disagreement with Mr Mead and built his own mill by the Icknield Way. The mill, without its sails, is now a private house.

The Oddy Hill goes up from Tring to Wigginton. The word 'oddy' was said to represent a type of Hertfordshire snail but a preferred version was that it meant a triangular headland, a shape it makes with the other road, the Twist. The Rothschild's summer house can be seen, in good condition, early this century. It was lived in during the last war by the actress, Peggy Ashcroft, but much has now sadly crumbled. What remains is being repaired and preserved.

The countryside along Duckmore Lane. This pair of cottages still stands at the fork. The left road leads to West Leith Farm and Stubbins Wood and straight on to Lord Rothschild's stud farm, Terriers End and Dancers End.

A view from the Oddy Hill. Taken around 1930, shows the Ivinghoe Beacon in the distance and, has changed little over the years.

The Upper Icknield Way, the ancient route that runs along the north side of the town, with the Ivinghoe Beacon in the background. This road to Dunstable and Whipsnade Zoo has also changed little over the years, though it is no longer suitable for cattle to walk along.

Left: Evans Spring, Hastoe Lane. Mrs Fulks sitting on the stile. *Right:* The Holloway, a very ancient track, goes up through Stubbins Wood from West Leith to Hastoe.

Left: Stubbins Wood started above Home Farm and ascended to Hastoe and along, as Pavis Wood, towards Paynes End. It was approached by a public footpath from Park Road, now diverted to Hastoe Lane, due to the building of the Tring bypass. *Right:* A view near Tring, the road to Dancers End. The house on the left was Gillinghams where sausage skins were made – it is said that, if the wind was in the wrong direction, the smell was awful.

An aerial view of Tring in the late 1960s. The museum can be seen in the top right hand corner. In the bottom right hand corner are the first buildings of Bishop Wood School but the old High Street School and the masters house are still there too. On the left, the market car park has not yet been built and the allotments to the left of the Black Horse pub are still there.

Moving in closer we can see the top of the Rose and Crown and the Nat-West and Midland Banks in the High Street. The Dolphin Square shopping precinct has yet to be built but the demolition of the area east of the church has started and only part of Church Lane and Westwood Lane remain.

34

Two
Shops and Businesses

Benjamin Saunders Gower ran the post office and general store, earlier this century, in New Mill and later set up a grocers and fruiterers shop in Western Road. This view, taken in the early 1950s, also shows Sketchley cleaners, now in the High Street, and Charles Atkin, baker.

Benjamin Kingham founded his cycle shop in the last decade of the nineteenth century, when cycling was in its pioneer days. His son, Reginald, can be seen in the photograph. When his wife died, Benjamin married for a second time, to Ellen Hopcroft, in 1904, and their son, Jack, later took over the business and ran it until he retired in 1971. Ellen lived to be Tring's first centenarian since the turn of the century and died in 1967 at the age of 101. In the photograph are: Horace Hedley Hopcroft, Benjamin Kingham, Reginald Kingham and an employee, thought to be Frank Batchelor.

Young Hedley Hopcroft tries out a motor bicycle from Kinghams Cycle Stores. The lane runs behind the shop in Western Road and the houses on the right hand side are one of four pairs of older houses in Goldfield Road.

John Gower and Son's waggon, photographed in 1910 at the junction of Brook Street and London Road. The Robin Hood can be seen on the left. The business was founded in 1876 and in the early 1900s was trading from premises in Queen Street and Western Road, dealing in coal, coke, wood and furniture removals. Before the First World War Gowers had sixteen horses but several of them were taken for war work. Travelling to Manchester or Leeds to make deliveries by rail the horses would be put in a horse box on the train and the pantechnicon on rolling stock.

James Hobbs the stonemasons in Western Road. The business was previously at Bottle Cross at the end of Park Road opposite the Britannia public house but was cleared away in the late 1880s. They then moved to Western Road and James Hobbs Senior can be seen there in this photograph taken around 1910. In 1891 forty-four-year-old James Snr, a widower, was living here with his son, also James, aged nineteen. James Jnr had two daughters, Mary and Fanny, and a son, Arthur.

Tring High Street, then called Western Road, in the early 1900s. On the right is Frederick Johnson's watchmakers shop. The 1891 census records him living there with his wife, Mary, and sixteen-year-old assistant Amos Gurney. In the shop next door Robert William Allison was a corn merchant and the business was still being run by his wife, Lucy, in the late 1930s. The sign above Frederick Waldock's bakers and confectioners can still be seen today as it was uncovered by the present proprietors, Jon Hall Interiors. Further down can be seen the Gazette Office and Cosier and Sons, high class tailors who moved to No. 35 High Street in the late 1930s. The man with the wheelbarrow is Joe 'Chops' and he is delivering coal.

As early as 1899 Kelly's listed Cash & Co., boot manufacturers in the Western Road. They were still there in 1937 but by then the road had been renamed, and they were now at No. 76 High Street. In this earlier photograph of around 1914 we see Mr Harlow standing outside the shop with his assistant Albert Prentice. The premises later became Turners shoe shop and more recently an estate agents. The library is now to the left.

Mr Edgar Bagnall stands in the doorway of his watchmaker and jewellers shop at 71 High Street. Edgar previously had a shop at 62 Akeman Street and around 1930 he moved up to the High Street or Western Road as it was called then. The shop was formerly the premises of Harry & Herbert Foskett, high class boot and shoe manufacturers. This photograph was taken by the present proprietor, Mr Brian Planton, when he took over the shop on Mr Bagnall's retirement in 1964.

The High Street Crossroads. Edward James Stevens cycle shop started in the early days of cycling and sold 'Yusemee' cycles which were made up on the premises. The shop was divided, with the cycle parts on one side and musical instruments and sheet music on the other; later, records and radios were introduced. This shop is now Arthur Starling's shoe shop but there is still a small department selling cycle parts. The shop on the corner, E. Gates and Son, sold tobacco, sweets, stationery and fancy goods. During the First World War it was run by Mrs Gates, and later by Arthur Gates, who also had a hairdressing business opposite at No.25a.

Mr George E. Goddard, a former railway inspector, purchased the confectionery and newsagents business at No.29 High Street, now The Wool Shop, in 1913, for £130. In 1925, his nephew, George William Goddard, bought the shop next door, No.28, and the business was transferred there in 1927. This photograph, taken in 1937, shows George William Goddard standing in the doorway of No.28.

Nos 31 and 32 High Street, here the premises of Robert Harrison & Sons. From the last century until the 1930s it was called Manchester House and was home to Richard Greening's tailors, drapers and clothiers business. Here, Tring people are queuing with their children to meet Father Christmas in the 1960s. The shop was later occupied by Charles Philips and Tescos, all self-service grocers, and now, considerably modernised, is the premises of the Woolwich.

Clements jewellers, watch and clockmakers. The Clement business started as far back as 1773 and stayed at 33 High Street until it closed down in the 1960s. No other firm in Tring had occupied the same premises for so long. The business has always serviced and repaired the clock mechanism in the parish church. In 1891 John Tripp Clement was the clock and watchmaker. A widower, he lived there with his children, two sons and five daughters, one of the sons being John Lovett, then eleven years of age.

Mr John Lovett Clement at his workbench behind his High Street shop. Mr Clement was an accomplished musician and as a young man he was the organist at the High Street Free Church. He was also a keen historian and his records of the past provide valuable information to those researching Tring's history. He was unmarried and when he retired the business closed. He died in 1964.

In the 1890s No.35 High Street was the premises of the International Tea Co. and around 1900 they moved to a shop next to Graces in Western Road, with Mr George Simpson as manager. This photograph shows William James Green, motor engineer and cycle maker, at No.35 High Street in around 1908. The sign tells us that they also had works in Harrow Yard, Akeman Street. Later the property was divided into two shops, and in the 1930s was occupied by Cosier & Sons, tailors, and The London Meat Co. Ltd. The shop is now a travel agency.

On the other side of the High Street, next to the old Tring Brewery arch, we have Sallery and Son, butchers. The business was in Akeman Street in 1882, at No.20, and in the early part of the twentieth century it was at 28 High Street, but a few years later it moved over the road to No.24. Three generations of the Sallery family had this butchers business, the last being Mr Reg Sallery who retired in around 1966. He was Tring's fire chief for ten years and a member of the fire brigade for twenty-one years. The butcher standing in the doorway is Derek Pike.

Wheeler Brothers, towards the lower end of the High Street, in the premises previously held by Ernest Kelsall Fulks drapers. Sidney Wheeler came from London in 1920, when this photograph was taken, and set up a drapery and men's outfitters business in partnership with his brother. Later his son, Ron, ran the shop until his retirement. There are now two businesses here, an estate agents and an opticians.

Mr Clarke and his staff outside his shop at No.19 High Street. Records show that as early as 1851 one Thomas Glover, aged twenty eight, and Joseph Gates, aged thirty-three, carried on a grocery business there, and it continued until well into the next century. Many Tring people still remember shopping at Glovers. The building is now a wine shop and also houses Tring's post office

Harry Johnson, fishmonger, Frogmore Street, now No.1 Parsonage Place. Mr Johnson is in the doorway of his shop. He moved there in the late 1890s from No.22 High Street. Much later in the century the business was run by William Keele, Mr Johnson's son in law. After Parsonage Place was redeveloped the shop then became a restaurant called 'Foxys' recently renamed 'Tringfellows'.

Mr George Sayer stands in the doorway of his barbers shop at No.12 Akeman Street. In the last century it had been occupied by Mrs Ellen Hill, a dressmaker. Records show that George was in business there in 1917 and stayed until the mid thirties; he was a keen musician and was bandmaster of the Salvation Army band. His son, Arthur, continued the business in premises a few doors away at No.9 Akeman Street. In 1937 his old shop was taken over by Ernest Childs, a boot and shoe repairer and some years later became a fish and chip shop.

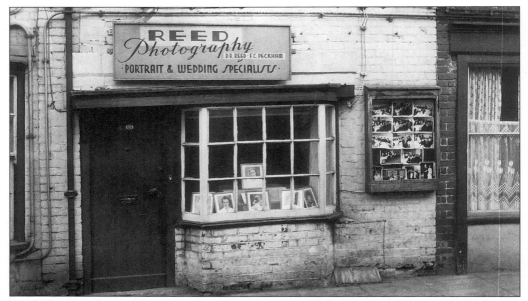

Reed Photography at No.13 Akeman Street in the 1950s. The shop has previously been a stationers, a fish shop, and a restaurant attached to the fish and chip shop when it was at No.12 next door. Soon after this photograph was taken, Don Reed took over the business on his own and expanded into the premises on the right, later opening shops in Chesham, Aylesbury and Banbury. The Tring branch closed in 1985 when the area was redeveloped and is now private houses. Don Reed retired from the photographic retail trade some years ago

Graces Mill, Akeman Street in the 1970s. It was a malting from medieval times until after the First World War. It continued as a corn mill for about another fifty years, run by Frank Grace and later by his sons Thomas and Robert. Tom and Bob were well known for their lantern slide shows of Old Tring, and Bob Grace still does them, but now with his niece Nuala. In the 1980s the mill was bought up by property developers who transformed the whole area into private dwellings, retaining only some of the original character of this historic building.

The interior of Grace's flour mill when it was still in use. The lower photograph shows the mill grinding the corn. The engine used to drive the mill can now be seen at the Pitstone Green Farm Museum.

Mead's flour mill at New Mill around 1900. The 1851 census tells us that William Mead, farmer and mill employer, was at Tring Wharf and was employing twenty workers. The windmill was demolished early this century.

Tring Dockyard and boat builders at New Mill. It was first owned by the Mead family who employed John Bushell to build and repair the canal boats which brought grain to their flour mill from the London docks and took back flour. From around 1875 his son Joseph developed the boatyard into a separate business, taking over from Meads in 1912, when Joseph's sons, Charlie and Joseph, were running it. The yard closed when they retired in 1952.

Three
At Work

Laying sewers in Langdon Street. Langdon Street from the Western Road end did not have much to inspire the photographer in the early part of the twentieth century. Cyril Howlett took this picture and it was produced as a postcard. The sewers, taken for granted these days, must have greatly improved the lives of local people.

The blacksmith's forge at No.51 High Street where Thomas Goodson and his son were the blacksmiths. In the next century George Stratford and Eric Reed were among the farriers who shod horses there.

The young man in the blacksmith's shop is Lionel Higby, then aged about seventeen. He was an employee of local farmer Mr Kingsley and had probably taken one of the horses to be shod.

Tring blacksmith, Eric Reed, with a heavy horse in the High Street forge. Born in 1884, and about sixty years old in this picture, Mr Reed cared for the feet of the zebras that Lord Rothschild trained to pull a pony trap. He served in Italy during the First World War as an armourer, repairing guns and shoeing horses.

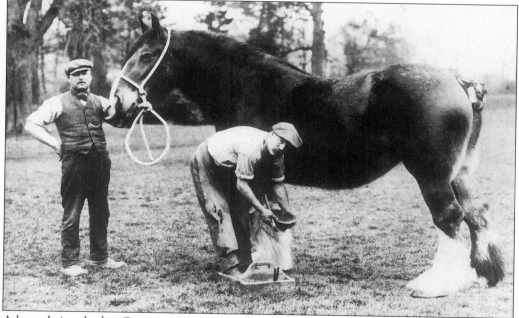

A horse being shod at Grove c. 1910. Albert Christopher is the blacksmith and holding the shire horse is Joe Croft who was the groom for Sir Gromer-Berry of Pendley Stock Farms. Mr Christopher lived in one of the West Leith cottages with his wife, Ann. She presented him with six sons, one of whom, Albert Christopher jnr, later worked as a chauffeur for Lord Rothschild.

Workers on Mr Kingsley's farm stop for a tea break. Left hand group: Fred Croft, Bert Flitney, Mr Seabrook. Centre: Len Fowler. Right hand group: -?-, Mr Kingsley, Lionel Higby (with dog).

Workers and local people by the remains of one of Tring's windmills. The mill, used by Meads flour mills, was by the canal at New Mill and was knocked down early this century. The man at the top is George Hall, who worked for Bushell Bros.

A rest while working on the road near Wilstone. The driver is unknown. In front are: Bill Dover, Harry Cartwright, Teddy Crockett, Eric Cartwright, Jack Oakley (road foreman), Harold Edwards, Bob James.

Estate workers pose in front of the huge bonfire built on the downs to celebrate the Coronation of King George V in 1911. It was constructed with great care, with the centre hollow so that it could be lit from the inside and would blaze for a considerable time.

Fireman tackling a fire at Mr Bob Grace's mill in Akeman Street in 1965. The fire, said to be caused by a grain dryer, destroyed the large grain store and drying machinery. Luckily it was prevented from spreading to the historic mill; now known as Graces Maltings. The central figure is Mr Grace.

This railway accident at Tring Station on 1 June 1908 was caused by wrongly set points. Twenty-seven coal trucks, that had come from Nuneaton, should have gone into a siding but went instead into the coal yard, crashing into about eighteen waggons which were already there. A seventeen-year-old boy named Higby, from Harrow Yard in Akeman Street, was crushed and killed instantly. Another lad named Butler was injured and was said by Dr. C. O'Keefe who attended the accident, to be suffering from shock. Also soon to arrive on the scene was Police Sergeant Baldock, from Tring, in response to a telegraph message from the station master. In the photograph the boy holding the shovel is Sydney Gower.

Four

Freetime

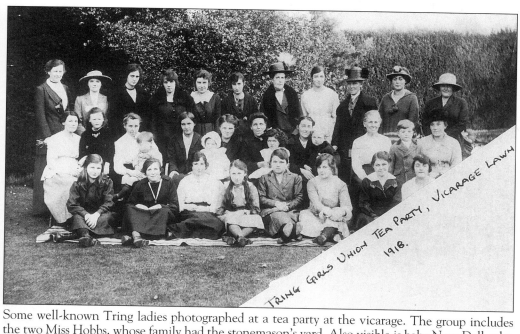

Some well-known Tring ladies photographed at a tea party at the vicarage. The group includes the two Miss Hobbs, whose family had the stonemason's yard. Also visible is baby Nora Dell, who later, as Mrs Nora Grace became well known in the town for her unstinting work with the Tring Red Cross, for which she was awarded the BEM. Back row, left to right: Miss Baines, Florrie Gomm, Mabel Fickin, Nancy Reeve, Florence Harding, Mary Hobbs, Mrs Morrison, Elsie Barber, Miss Elliman, Alice Dye, Bess Newcon. Middle row: Alice Waterton, Gwen Waterton, Mrs Rance and son, Annie Collier, Mrs Dell and daughter Nora, Mrs Randall and daughter Florence, Miss Primett, -?-, Mrs Collins, Stan Fletcher, Mrs Fletcher. Front row: Doris Gomm, Fanny Hobbs, Edie Jennings, -?-, Cis Howlett, Ivy Lee, Kath Collins, Dorothy Newcon.

Tring YMCA Gymnast Team. Back row: Sid Lovell M, Sid Horn, Arthur Church, ? Swaby (Aldbury), Frank Bly, -?-, -?-, -?-, Bill Budd, -?-. Third row: 'Decko' Budd, ? Gomm, John Prentice. Second row: Jack Lines, Stan Minall, Mac Rush, ? Wright, -?-, ? Budd, Gillie Rance. Front row: Joe Lovell, ? Poulton, Jack Kingham, ? Collins, -?-, ? Bligh, Bobbie Bell.

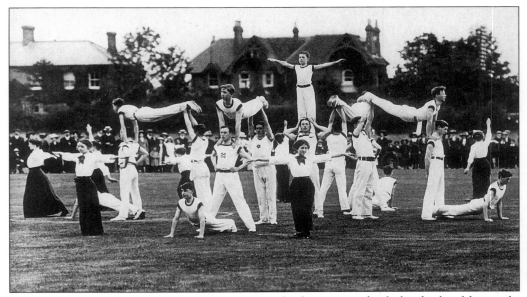

In June 1914 the YMCA team gave a gymnastic display to raise funds for the local hospitals. The ground is that of the Tring Park Cricket Club and Station Road can be seen in the background.

Mr Frederick Reeve with his group of bell ringers outside Tring church. Back row: -?-, Harry Bull, Visiting ringer, Chris Badrick, Visiting ringer, ? Cherry?, Harold Brackley, Jesse Puplett, Harry Jones, Front row: -?-, Frederick Reeve, Nathan Brackley. Mr Frederick James Reeve was born in Tring in 1873. He was an enthusiastic bell-ringer for most of his life and travelled all over England visiting other churches and joining their teams ringing different bells. He was also a member of Tring Fire Brigade, which he joined in 1912.

Akeman Street Baptist church outing to the Wembley Exhibition of 1924. The charabanc was supplied by Mr Prentice from Western Road. Back row: (standing and sitting) Dorothy Wright, Frank Bly, -?-, Rose West, Miss Ginny West, Miss Osbourne, Miss Fincher, John 'Tommy' Chapman, Cissie Chapman, Front row: Mr Hedges, Harold Howlett, Phyllis Howlett, Miss King, Alice Smith, Mrs Smith, Mr Fincher, Miss Olive Foskett, Mrs Fincher, (small boy) Bobby Fincher, Nellie Reeve, -?-, -?-, Daisy Hedges, Lily Hedges, Miss Hedges. In front: (boy) Alfred Wright, Mr Sidney Garrad (pastor of chapel), Driver -?-.

A Sunday School group early this century walking up Langdon Street on their way to Tring park, where they would play games and enjoy a picnic. These houses look much the same today. The turning into Charles Street on the left can just be seen in the distance, with the Co-operative Stores, butchers and bakery on the corner, now converted into private dwellings. Just this side can be seen the railings of the Methodist Church, now demolished and replaced by a pair of semi-detached houses.

A coach outing for members of New Mill Baptist Church in the 1930s. The lady on the left hand side in the front row is Mrs Welling, whose husband was a member of the Tring Fire Brigade for many years. Just beyond her on the back row the hatless man is Mr Dando, the Baptist minister and further along the line are Mr and Mrs Randall, Charlie Wilkins, Mrs Welling and Albert Christopher.

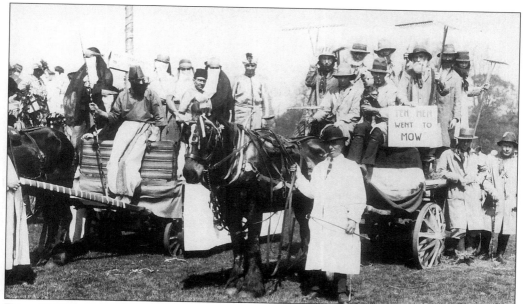

Tring YMCA floats in Tring Park for the Jubilee Day Celebrations in 1935. The man in the dark fez on the left hand float is 'Nobby' Rance, well known in Tring as he was the manager of the Charles Street Co-op. The Man in the Indian costume is Frank Bly. On the other float are: Roland Rance, George Christopher, Fred Waterton, Wally Rance, Bert Wright, and 'Knock' Higby with dog. Standing by the float are Frank Johnson and Harold Brackley. Standing by the horse is Billy Mills.

Another YMCA float with: Len Lovegrove (Australian), Stanley Fletcher (Britannia), Archie Fulks (John Bull), Bert Wright and Stanley Wright (each side of John Bull). The man holding the horse is Marsworth-born, Dennis Johnson.

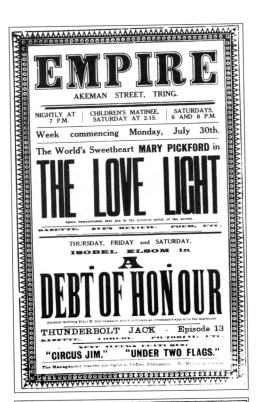

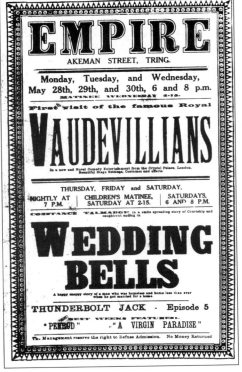

Posters for films shown at the Empire Picture Palace Theatre in Akeman Street in the early 1920s. The Empire opened in 1916 only a few days before the rival Gem in Western Road. The Gem only survived for a few years and the Empire, renamed the Gaiety in 1932, remained the only cinema until the Regal was opened in Western Road in 1936. This had a severe effect and the Gaiety's popularity waned, but it did not close until war broke out in 1939. The building is still there, used as business premises.

The site of the first Gem cinema in the lower High Street, where Tring's first cinema was opened in 1912. The Unity Hall was above the Tring Co-op. It held 300 people and, with a 19-foot-deep stage, was often used for plays. Alterations were made and it was turned into the Gem picture hall, with P.J. Darvell the licensee. He later built a new Gem cinema in Western Road, but this did not survive for long, as at the same time the Empire was being built in Akeman Street, and the Gem closed in the early 1920s. These premises, still marked Unity Hall on the doorway, are now the Frances Elizabeth Crystal Rooms, used for banquets and wedding receptions.

The Regal cinema opened on 10 September 1936. It did very good business during the Second Wold War, the population of Tring being swelled by evacuees from London and the American forces stationed at Marsworth. It did less well later, due to competition from Aylesbury and Hemel Hempstead and closed in 1958, the last film shown being *Gunfight at the OK Corral*. Efforts were made for further projects, both with cinema and live theatre, but by the end of 1978 the building was demolished and ten flats where built on the site and given the name Regal Court.

Tring Town Football Club. Back row: Arthur 'Junky' Baldwin, Bert Hare, 'Choice' Higby, Jimmy Webb, 'Butler' Howlett. Middle row: Doug Westcroft, Fred Reeves, Stan Hart. Front row: ? Gomm, Tony Musgrave, George Connell, 'Chuckle' Brooks, Bob Cato.

Tring Park Cricket Club 1920 First XI. Back row: H. Challen (scorer), Leonard Hawkins, Reg Honour, Harold Saunders, Arthur Hedges, D. Hart, Mr Prior (umpire). Middle row: 'Teddy' Clarke, Arthur Butcher (captain), C.P. Cole. Front row: Tom Blundell, George Bell, Revd T.V. Garnier, T. Pratt.

Tring Park Cricket Club 1932 Wednesday XI. The Wednesday XI consisted of players who had local shops or businesses that involved having to work on a Saturday. Standing: L. Brooks (scorer), Albert Kempster, Harry Baker, L. King, Horace Bandy, Reg Sallery, A. Fulks, C. Batchelor (umpire). Sitting: S. Lovegrove, Arthur Waldock, Fred Cox (captain), R. Cosier, Jack Kingham.

The Tring Park Cricket Club 1951 Second XI. Back row: R. Darwin (umpire), Stan Scales, F. Wilson, H. Dixon, P. Earner, Bill Green, F. Fisk. Sitting: C. Batchelor, William Kew, Fred Howlett (captain), Doug Westcott, L. Corbett. Front: L. Hitchings (scorer).

The Tring Girl Guides at their camp site at Hang Hill, near Tring, during the Second World War. Some of these girls came to Tring as evacuees at the beginning of the war. Back row: Miss Howson, Lily Jaycock, Hazel Bowman, Barbara Verney, Joan Killick, Betty Warwick, Joyce Rowe, Joan Wright, Pamela Nye, Elaine Berry, Jean Singer?, Barbara Heath, Jill Walters, Thelma Nye, Florence Goddard. Front row: Ruth Norman, Frances Bellamy, Josie Simmons, Peggy Warwick, Janice Gower, Christine List.

Cubs and scouts at the Chiltern Bus Company's Tring Garage in Western Road on Saturday, 1 July 1933, waiting to go to the County Rally at Hatfield House. The rally was to welcome the Chief Scout and Lady Baden-Powell. In charge was SM. Nicol Stenhouse and some of the boys were J. Tarmer, L. Symons, J. Deverill, J. Howlett, Rover Squires, ? Duff, ? Lawrence, ? Brady, L. Tarmer, ? Plum, Mr Wright of Wright & Wright kindly lent a van free of charge to take the troop's gear.

1st Tring Scout Group in front of the bonfire they built for the Silver Jubilee celebrations in May 1935, on the downs above Tring.

1st Tring Scout Group at Kingsdown summer camp 1955. Back row: Roland Jeffery, Leslie Horne, Ralph Wood, Len Cousins, Phil Gibbs, Trevor Ellis, Robert Collins, Alan Horne, Mervyn Bone, Roger Evans, Malcolm Hewitt, Pat Deverell, Jack Kingham. Front row: Ron Kindel, Terry Childs, Keith Crannage, Dave West, Eddie Golightly, Derek Read, David Gunn, Tony Read.

The British Legion band and members, some in fancy dress, parade down the High Street, in 1935, on their way to the Park for their fete. Mr George Sayer was Bandmaster and Mr A.G Crocker and Mrs E.A. Rance carried the standards. The policeman is standing on the corner where, for many years, you would not have been able to take a photograph without including a member of Tring's police force.

The Tring British Legion band photographed here in full uniform for the first time, after taking part in the special church parade in connection with the Patronal Festival of Tring parish church in 1934. Back, by the flag: ? Bradding, -?-. Back row, standing: ? Goodall, Stan Barber, ? Copcutt, -?-, -?-, Albert Clarkson, George Sayer (bandmaster), -?-, Sid Lovegrove, ? Booth, ? Cooper, Fred Baldwin, ? Rance, George Bradding. Front row, sitting: Ray Sayer, -?-, ? Palmer, Arthur Bradding, -?-, Sam Marshall, Fred Copcutt, ? Hearn, G. Doody, Jack Hearn. Front row boys: A. Copcutt, -?-.

This photograph was taken around 1929 by the local photographer, Mr George Bell. While out for a walk he met the 'Henry Street Gang' and persuaded them to pose for his camera. They are: (at back) Ernest Foster, Len Smith, Gary Harrop, Arthur Keen, Alfie Hearn, Ken Smith, Phillip Keen, Len Collins, Les Foster.

A group of Tring people at the 'Old Tyme Market' held in the High Street in 1952. Adults: Fanny Mead, Mrs Hollands, Freddie Welch, Nora Grace, Ann ?. Children: Janet ? , Heather Grace, Ann Grace, John Grace, Ann ? . In the background can be seen Bob Metcalfe and Tom Grace.

Tring Young Wives outing in 1955. Back row: Mrs C. Organ, Mrs Lila Jennings , Mrs 'Snowy' Hewett, Mrs Lisa Lockhart, Mrs Organ's mother, Mrs Tite, Mrs Bishop, -?-, Mrs G Hall. Front row: Mrs Eirlys Thomas, Mrs Peggy Slemeck, Mrs Janie Standen, Mrs Grace Hodge, Mrs Connie Wright, Mrs Molly Benson, Mrs Kath Jelly.

There was a Tring Camera Club in the early years of this century, as existing prize medals of the time show. It was obviously dissolved later and was not revived until the early 1960s, when the members met in the Hall in Tabernacle Yard in Akeman Street. They now meet in the Vestry Hall. This photograph shows a portrait session in the late sixties. Those with cameras are: Leslie Bristow, Len Coulham, Dave Kingham, Neville Pearman, and Hugh Bass. Others in the group are Dick Bignell, Melvin Nash, John Waterton, Margaret Bass, Bob Hummer, and Robert Vickers.

Five
Schooldays

A pre-1920s photograph of Tring schoolboys. The group includes: Bob Potter, Fred Reeve, G. Bradding, W. Gomm, ? Higby, ? Hearn, Reg Potter and S. Hearn. Bob and Reg Potter later had a shop in the High Street selling paints and decorating materials.

An early photograph of Ivy Cottage, Miss Wilson's 'dame school' in Western Road. It was there before the National School and schoolmaster's house that can be seen in the background. The children would have been taught the skills of straw plaiting. The gate on the right is the entrance to Parsonage Farm.

A later view of Ivy Cottage, then occupied by Thomas Pusey. In the doorway we see Mr Pusey, a widower, who lived in the cottage with his granddaughter, Annie. He was the estate carpenter for Pendley and his workshop can be seen on the left.

Prospect House School in the 1890s, viewed from the downs. To the left are houses in Park Road and to the right the Louisa Cottages, when only the first part had been built, and beyond them is the Museum. Prospect House was demolished as part of the Rothschild clearance scheme and the site is now an open field for horse grazing.

A closer view of Prospect House School. This was a thriving boys school maintaining a high standard of education. Dr Clarabut, the New Mill pastor, was headmaster, followed by Mr Mark Young. In the 1891 census the school had eleven boarders, most coming from London and the home counties. When the buildings were demolished the school was moved to Brookfield, when the headmaster was Mr Maull.

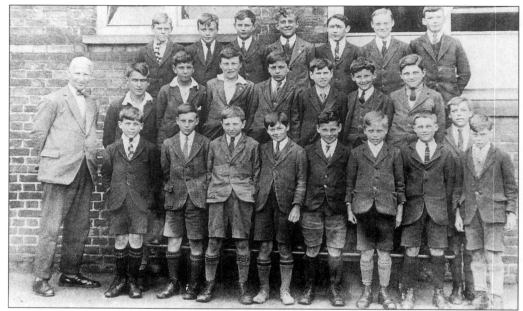

A class of Tring School in the 1920s. The master is Mr Douglas Harrison. He came to the school in 1925 and was appointed headmaster of Tring Church of England mixed school in 1931. He died in 1942 shortly after his retirement. Back row: Cyril Batchelor, Charlie Kempster, William Budd, George Prentice, William Barber, Harold Bowley, Henry Porter Christopher. Middle row: Lionel Tyrrel, Roland Austin: Jack Harding, Charles Mildred, Les Picton, Wally Crockett, Harold Randall. Front row: Maurice Mansfield, Joseph Edwin, Jack Ide, B. Miller, C. Paget, Charlie Kempster. William Edwin, ? Nutkins, George Ginger.

Tring schoolboys c. 1926-7. Back row: Dicky Brandon, Peter Rush, Sidney Bullock, Joe Brooks, Ian Marks, Bob Fincher, Frank Gower, G. Smith, Dave Davis, Donald Theed, Basil Everett, Peter Bell. Middle row: A. Watkins, C. Knapp, Albert Higby, A. Caldwell, F. Witson, Charles Blundell, Les Tarmer, Tony Griffin, Harold Wilkins, Graham Clarkson, Peter Bowley. Front row: A. Cross, Ron Emery, Charles Meek, Reg West, Willy Messenger, Jack Ives, Logan Tapping, Cyril Ginger, Steb Allibone, Chris Batchelor, Sidney Eldridge.

Tring junior mixed scholarship winners of 1936. Back row: Miss Smith, Miss Baker, Miss Lacey. Middle row: Arthur Haddon, John Vranch, ? Perkins, John Chapman, Peter Harrowell. Front row: Audrey Mansfield, Barbara Kettle, Vera Gurney, Terry Buckingham.

Tring School group of 1950. Back row: Mr Hamilton, ? Smith, Vicky Collins, Enid Hill, -?-, -?-, Pam Chandler, -?-, Ann Kempster, Neville Kempster, Brian Dover, Miss Baker. Middle row: -?-, Annie Gascoine, David Kempster, Michael Colby, Paddy Foster, June Welling, Michael Bond, ? Rance, Bruce Messenger, Mavis Fleckney. Front Row: Brenda Mills, John Ashpool, Robin ?, Audrey Bingham, Ann Wright, Leslie Chamberlain, Brenda Lee, -?-, Sadie Wright.

Class of Tring School in the late 1940s with teacher Mr Les Tarmer. Back row: Phyllis Hart, Pamela Burney, Jean Sayer, Ken Verney, Stephen Hearn, Pamela Sheen, Eunice Wander, June Flitney. Third row: Joe Kempster, Dennis Gunn, Alan Rance, Derek Freeman, Alfie Welling, Brian Mortlock, Dennis Burch. Second row: Evelyn Keen, Marion Burch, Gwen Weedon, Maureen Green, Mavis Rance, Mary Bethell, Avis Butler. Front row: Clive Halsey, Ray Smith, John Drake, Harry Jeffs, Kenny Rance, Peter Flitney, Michael Cox.

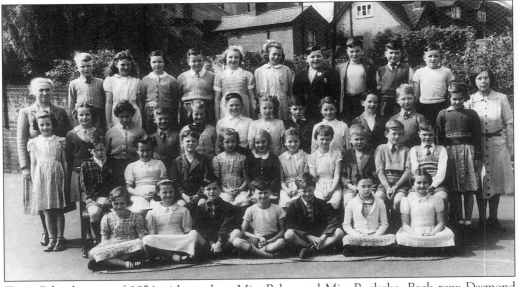

Tring School group of 1954 with teachers Miss Baker and Miss Buckoke. Back row: Desmond Anning, Heather Halsey, Frances Lowdell, Tony Baker, Marion Ginger, Sandra Hearn, Barry Webster, Barry Wells, Andy McCallister, Jimmy Carter, Third row: -?-, Jill Organ, Janine Mitchell, David Everton, -?-, ? Higby, -?-, -?-, -?-, -?-, Brian Gregory, -?-, Second row: Alan Smith, Angela Bateman, Raymond Huey, -?-, Jean Nash, -?-, Brenda Smith, Paul Wright, Michael Standen, -?-. Front row: Pamela Philpott, -?-, Terry Ives, David Major, -?-, -?-, Christine Cousens.

Tring Junior School in 1956 with their teacher Mrs Hamilton. Back row: Adam Wainwright, Graham Broad, Derek Hearn, Andrew ?, Alan Lawrence, Bill Dwight, Steven Gregory, Frankie Phillips, Gareth Noble. Third row: Susan Elliot, Jacqueline Barnes, Ann Garrett, Mary Hinton, Elizabeth Miller, Lynn Wright, Terry Oliver, Simon Warren, Second row: Penny Standen, Hilary Prouse, Doreen Pearsall, Valerie ?, Beryl Verney, Linda Hoare, Sally Jones, Annette Seabrook, Christine Chapman. Front row: John Nutkins, Graham ?, Geoffrey Gort, Nicholas Harris, Benjamin ?, Alistair Keay, -?-, Nigel Rodwell, Anthony Hartley.

Tring School group with teachers Mr and Mrs Stanley Thomas. Back row: Derek Stratton, Raymond Hooper, Roland Ginger, Alan Horne, Stephen Humphreys, Robin Desborough, Barry Wooton, Richard Stratford. Middle row: Susan Pitcher, Brian Johnson, Keith Messenger, David Prentice, Les Casemore, John Cutler, Ian Johnson, Robert Denby. Front row: -?-, Shirley Bailey, Dean Horne, Sheila Simmonds, Kay Jelley, Jill Campbell, Pat Newton, Brenda Deeley, Pamela Worrall.

Junior school children in the 1970s playing outside the schoolmaster's house when the school was still in the High Street. This house and the school were later demolished and replaced by the library and car park.

At Tring School, the popular headmaster, Mr Stanley Thomas, is being given a noisy send-off by his pupils on his retirement in 1968. With him is his wife, Eirlys, who still lives in Tring and is remembered affectionately by many ex-pupils, as she was also one of the school's teachers.

An aerial view of the old High Street School and the masters house, showing the new Bishop Wood School in the background. The old buildings were later demolished to make way for the new library.

When the new school was built to replace the old High Street building, a small swimming pool was included, here being enjoyed by some young pupils. When the larger indoor pool was built at the senior school at Mortimer Hill, available to the public out of school hours, the use of this one was discontinued.

Popular school teacher Bob Hummer, with a group of his pupils at Bishop Wood School. As well as his school interests, Bob devoted a lot of his spare time to the Tring Scouts and was Scoutmaster for many years. He was also a very keen photographer, taking several of the photographs in this book, and was Chairman of Tring Camera Club from its early days, a position he held for the rest of his life. Some of the children pictured here are Paul Gilson, Stephen Adams, Ian Scott and Tim Dureall.

Early days of the Secondary Modern School at Mortimer Hill. A lot of the buildings in this 1955 photograph are temporary huts which were later replaced by the brick ones that stand today. Here the flourishing school garden can be seen before it made way for more buildings and tennis courts. Now the school is almost surrounded by housing estates.

Six

Churches
and Places of Worship

Tring Parish Church in the 1960s. Parts of the church date back to the fifteenth century, though most has been added to over the years and major restorations were done in the nineteenth century. A striking monument in the north aisle is that of Sir William and Lady Gore of Tring Park. Sir William is dressed in the robes of the Lord Mayor of London.

The interior of Tring church. The pews in the nave were made in the 1860s by James Forsyth of London, who also made the pulpit which was given by former patrons, the students of Christ Church College, Oxford. Most of the stained glass windows are by the famous Victorian firm of C.E. Kempe.

The Old vicarage was built in Victorian times but in a mock Jacobean style. In 1891, the Vicar in residence was the Revd William Quennell, a widower, who lived with his sister and daughter. It was purchased by the Sutton Housing Trust and remains virtually unaltered. Buildings were added to make the Trust's offices and the Anglican-Methodist hall. The complex won the Royal Institute of British Architects award in 1976.

The Baptist Chapel. One of the earliest in Hertfordshire, the first chapel was built at Frogmore End, now Frogmore Street, in 1751. It was described as 'one of the queerest, stuffiest, ugliest little chapels you can conceive of. It has a grave yard in front which the road turns to avoid'. In the late 1830s the building was enlarged to front the road and here in the 1970s is being used as an antique shop. It is now a private house.

A new Baptist church was built late in the nineteenth century in the High Street. Many ministers served their communities for a considerable number of years including the Revd William Sexton (1838-1874) and the Revd Charles Pearce (1874-1920). The United Free Baptist Church, completed in 1886 comprised a church and lecture hall, and a new organ was bought in 1949 to replace one that had been there since the beginning of the century.

The Quaker Meeting House at the end of Akeman Street, in Park Street. There were Quakers in Tring in the seventeenth century but they suffered considerable persecution. By the cottage was a burial ground where some eighty Quakers were buried. The cottage was demolished in the nineteenth century and all that remains now is the ground with a monument inscribed: ' This enclosure was used by the Society of Friends as a burying ground from 1678-1809'. 'In our church is neither epitaph nor monument, tombstone nor names, only the turf we tread and a few natural graves' (Wordsworth).

The Tring Salvation Army band c. 1930. Back row: Stan Barber, Albert Hart, Arthur Brown (flagman), George Baker, George Smith (RAF Halton). Third row: Frank Gascoine, Ray Sayer, Will Gascoine, Harold Sayer, George Sayer (bandmaster), J. Finney, Mr McCurdy, George Impey. Second row: Miss Daisy Gascoine, -?-, -?-, -?-. Front row: Jim Impey, Arthur Sayer. A Salvation Army band still plays in the town and they meet in their citadel in Albert Street.

Akeman Street Baptist Chapel from a drawing of 1808 when the meeting house was built. Pastor Glover made the chapel very popular and it became known as 'Glovers Chapel', attracting members from the New Mill Chapel. The building has been enlarged and improved but looks much the same and is still in regular use as a place of worship.

St Marthas church was built around 1880, probably by Carpenter and Ingelow who were at the time working on the parish church. In the early 1900s the west arm was built with dark weatherboarding, and much later a brick porch was added. It was later registered for Methodist marriages, the first wedding being that of Miss Susan Wilshire on 26 January 1974. The big tree was a victim of the gales in January 1990.

The Primitive Methodist chapel in Langdon Street was built in the latter half of the nineteenth century, the stone-laying ceremony taking place on 22 September 1870. Although the membership was not very large and the chapel suffered bomb damage in the Second World War, the church reached its centenary in 1970 and there were two weeks of celebrations. Sadly, soon after that, it was decided that the membership could not continue to finance the repairs that were necessary, and when the Langdon Street Methodists were invited, in 1975, to share St Marthas in Park Road with the Anglicans, they were pleased to do so. After the demolition of the chapel a pair of semi-detached houses were built to fill the space.

New Mill Baptist Church. There are records to suggest that Baptists worshipped in New Mill in the seventeenth century but the first chapel was built in 1775, when Henry Blaine was the minister. In 1818, when Daniel Clarabut was pastor, the present church was built and a school room, which can be seen behind it, was built in 1897. The photograph was taken very early this century.

Seven

Services

This horse-drawn fire engine was in use for almost 200 years, not being replaced by a motorised model until the 1930s. The horses belonged to Mr Gower, the coal merchant, who is here seen driving them.

Here the Tring Fire Brigade, and members of the council, pose by their new Model T Ford fire engine. Back row: -?-, Duke Welling. Middle row: Mr Reeves, Edward Brittain, Fred Rance, Bill Cooper, -?-, George Putnam, Bill Keele, -?-. Front row: Mr W.N. Mead, -?-, John Bagnall, John Bly, -?-, Hubert Gurney (seated) Clerk of the Council, Mr Baldock (ex PC), George Goddard.

Tring Fire Brigade with their new Leyland fire engine photographed at the Silk Mill in Brook Street. Top row: Eddie Brackley, -?-, Bertie Wright. Middle row: George Hinton, Sid Lovell, William Keele, George Goodliffe. Front row: Mr Sear, S. Harrop, William Welling, George Putnam, Fred Rance, W. Richardson, Harry Bull.

A line up of Tring firemen being presented with long service medals by the Chairman of the Council, Capt. 'Donald' Brown (he was called Macdonald but was always known as 'Donald'). Front row: William Keele, Eddie Brackley, Harry Bull, George Hinton, Sid Lovell, William Welling. In the back row are: George Goodliffe (concealed behind Mr Keele), S. Harrop, Fred Rance. At the front: Captain George Putnam.

Tring Fire Brigade outside the purpose-built station in Brook Street, and behind is the new Bedford fire engine. When the station was in the Market House, on the corner of Akeman Street, the entrance was so narrow that this fire engine was fitted with rubber bumpers to protect it from scratches. Left to right: Jock Graffen, Ken Carlisle, Bill Giddings, Doug Sinclair, Paddy Foster, Charlie Cummings, Tom Saunders, Roy Robinson, Wally Rance, Dennis Bradding, Dudley Fulks, John Foskett, Bill Gosling.

Tring and District 'Special' Police in 1940s. Back row: -?-, George Evans, -?-, -?-, William Jeffery, Mr Hamilton, Eric Mead, Arthur Edwards. Middle row: -?-, Frank Rogers, -?-, -?-, -?-, Percy Bagnall, -?-, Stanley Thomas, R. George Wright. Front row. Starmer Collins, -?-, Harold Grace, Charles Bushell, -?-, -?-, Tom Pratt, Jack Wright, -?-, Mr Green.

Tring Red Cross 1946. Back row: Mrs Badrick, Molly Newman, -?-, Agnes Gurney, Gertrude Jones, Hilda Tyler, Gladys Hull, Nora Grace, -?-, Betty Dell, Gladys Cato, Mrs McDermott. Middle row: -?-, Mrs Mead, Miss Bowlby, -?-, Elsie Batchelor, Mrs Chapman, Mrs Simmonds, Kathy Akers, Joyce Warwick, Lily Jaycock, Gladys Price, Mrs Carrington, Mrs Cartwright (Wilstone). Front row: Mrs Rolfe, Mrs Flower, Joan Cole, Dr. Knox, Phyllis Wright, Mary Bowlby, Dolly Keen, Mrs Marshall, Mrs Scaby.

Tring St John Ambulance Brigade in the 1940s. Back row: Tom Hedges, George Bell, John Copcutt, Bill Capel, Peter Capel, Wally Rance, Stan Harrop, Mr Budd, Mr Bagnall. Front row: Doug Saunders, Tom Moy, Jock Blyth, -?-, Frank Rance.

Young members of the Red Cross, c. 1960. Back row: Rosemary Prentice, Geraldine Gordon, Margaret Kempson, Janet Lovell, Susan Sayer, Jacqueline Kempster, Rosemary Stone, Evelyn Tippett, Janet Reeves, -?-. Front row: Penelope Southgate, -?-, Mrs Whittaker, Rosemary Hamilton, Delia ?.

The Tring Council water carrier, with Billy Mills, filling up at the water hydrant in Charles Street. The shop in the background is a drapers, ran for many years by Miss Ives. It is now a private house.

Having filled up the tank the carrier can be seen laying the dust in Tring High Street. On a hot day the children would follow the cart to enjoy a cool shower. On the right of the photograph can be seen part of the Rose and Crown Hotel.

Eight

Tring Park
and the Rothschilds

The gates to Tring Park decorated to welcome Nathaniel Rothschild's younger son, Charles, and his bride, Hungarian-born Rozsika von Wertheimstein, after their marriage in 1907. Rozsika was an athletic young lady, she was the Hungarian lawn tennis champion and an accomplished ice skater, but she settled down well in England and she and Charles had four children. The eldest daughter, Miriam, is well known as a biologist, interested in flora and fauna, as her Uncle Walter had been, and also for her writings about the Rothschild families.

The Tring Park gates from the inside, showing the High Street in the background. These beautiful gates, made by Gilbert Grace, sadly went for scrap during the Second World War. Notice on the left hand side the Old Market House still stands in front of the church. The shop with the blinds down is Ellimans, drapers and agents for the County Fire Insurance Co.

The Park Street entrance to the mansion. The iron gates have now gone, another casualty of the war effort, but the gate house and the other houses still remain. Alongside the gate house runs the public footpath to the park, now under management of the Woodland Trust, having been purchased by Dacorum Borough Council in 1994, 'to preserve it for the people of Tring, as a historic parkland and an important part of the Chiltern countryside'.

The mansion as it was before its purchase by the Rothschilds. It was built for Henry Guy, groom of the bedchamber to King Charles II and is attributed to Sir Christopher Wren. The Tring Park Estate was sold to Baron Lionel de Rothschild for £230,000 in 1872.

Tring mansion after Baron Rothschild had it altered more to his taste, a sort of 'cladding' over the original building, and another wing was added. It was not to everyone's liking and was described by some as looking like a large hospital and a well-windowed Victorian prison. It is now home of the Arts Educational School and is virtually unaltered.

The two members of the Rothschild family who had the greatest influence on Tring. Seen here on his hunter is Nathaniel Mayer (1840-1915) who built a lot of the town as it still is today, and his son Lionel Walter (1868-1937), here in his sixties, who founded the world famous museum.

Tring Museum after it was opened to the public in 1892. The cottage in front is that of Mr Alfred Minall, Walter Rothschild's taxidermist, and his family. It was built by Walter's father as part of his coming-of-age present. Walter, when only twelve years of age, dreamed of having his own museum and in 1880 made Alfred Minall his curator, with his workshop in Albert Street.

The Bothy on the London Road when it was used by Lord Rothschild's gardeners. The word 'bothy', dating back to the eighteenth century, is said to mean 'a small hut or cottage, especially for housing labourers'. This does not adequately describe this building which was well built and survives to this day, although its future may be at risk if plans for a supermarket on the site go ahead.

Tring Show in Tring Park. The history of Tring Show dates back to 1841 but it started in a very small way at Tring station, later moving to the Park. It was originally held in October but was changed to August in the first Lord Rothschild's time and by then was attracting around 20,000 visitors.

Lord Rothschild was particularly interested in the breeding of heavy horses and had a stud farm outside Tring, where Thomas Fowler was in charge. Here several elegant ladies are watching the heavy horse class at Tring Show, but the show programme stated that the mansion gardens would be open for the enjoyment of those ladies not interested in agricultural matters. There was also a barber available for the gentleman.

Tring Show became the largest one day show in the country and there were classes for all types of farm animals as well as dog trials and show jumping. The show was not held in Tring Park after 1939.

Lord Rothschild's stud farm at West Leith in the countryside outside Tring. These buildings have now been converted into comfortable private houses.

Town Farm, where Mr Dawe lived, provided the site where Lord Rothschild built Home Farm for his agent Mr Richardson Carr.

Home Farm photographed in the 1950s when it housed the Moss family. It was the home of Lord Walter Rothschild for the last few years, before his death in 1937. During the Second World War it was used as a maternity home run by volunteers. After the war it was sold to Flight-Lieutenant Kirby, who made various additions, including an ornamental pool with a fountain and two life-size female figures, all built in the centre of the farm yard.

Mr Richardson Carr, photographed at a sale in the farmyard; he was the agent for the estate and the occupant of Home Farm. The 1891 census lists him, aged thirty four, with his wife, Mary, daughter Catherine, then aged eight, and three servants. The roadway to the house is still known to older people as 'Carr's Drive'.

Tring has had several well known citizens, but perhaps none more famous than Stirling and Pat Moss who lived at Home Farm, then renamed White Cloud Farm. Stirling, the top racing driver of his day, was the first Briton to win the Mille Miglia, in May 1955, and won his first Grand Prix two months later. In July 1957 he won the British Grand Prix at Aintree, the first Britain to do so since 1923, and in the same year won the Italian Grand Prix at Monza. Pat, equally well known in the showjumping world, was the 'Leading Juvenile Jumper of the Year' at Harringay in 1950 on her pony 'Brandy of White Cloud'. She progressed to senior jumping and was with the British Team for fifteen years, two of her best horses being 'Geronimo' and 'Danny Boy'. She combined riding with rally-driving and was European Champion for six years; later giving up show jumping to concentrate on driving.

Nine
Tring in the Wars

Father Christmas distributing gifts to the evacuees in Albert Street in 1939. The little boy in the spotted hat is Charlie 'Tarpy' Rance; the identities of the twin girls and Father Christmas are not known. The boy and girl behind Santa are brother and sister Doug and Mavis Sinclair, the boy with fair hair in front of Mavis is brother Peter Sinclair. The boy in the dark cap is? Brandon, and the boy in front with the light cap is David Mills. The boy on the far right is Ivor Mills.

Although Private 'Jacko' Osborne served with the 58th Northamptonshire Regiment and was the first soldier in the regiment to win the Victoria Cross, his funeral took place in Wigginton as he had lived there for so many years. He won his VC at Wesselroom in 1881 during the Boer War. He died in 1928 aged seventy-one. The photograph shows the coffin being loaded on a gun carriage by six pall bearers from the 2nd Northamptonshire Regiment with almost everyone in the village turning out to see the event. The Revd T. Drake conducted the service in the church.

Dedication of the memorial to Private James Osborne VC. The group include Mr and Mrs Poulton, Private Osborne's daughter and son-in-law with their baby. During the Boer War Private Osborne was sent out with a friend, Private Mayes, and another soldier to cut some forage for the horses when the Boers attacked them. Private Mayes horse was killed and he was shot in the leg. The other man was shot dead. Private Osborne galloped back to the camp but finding that Private Mayes had not followed he galloped back, picked up his wounded comrade and, miraculously avoiding bullets, got them both safely back. Both soldiers survived the rest of the war and although Private Mayes died before Private Osborne, his two children, Mr George Mayes and Mrs J.H. Brookes, attended the funeral at Wigginton.

Private Edward Barber VC was in the 1st Battalion Grenadier Guards and was the son of William and Sarah Ann Barber and was the only Tring-born soldier to receive the Victoria Cross. The award was for his conspicuous bravery at Neave Chappell on 12 March 1915. The citation reads: 'He ran speedily in front of the Grenade Company, to which he belonged and threw bombs at the enemy with such effect that a very large number of German soldiers at once surrendered. When the grenade party reached Private Barber they found him quite alone and unsupported with the enemy surrendering all around him'. He did not know of his award, however, as he was killed in action the same day, said to have been 'picked off by a German sniper'.

Digging for the Second World War air raid shelters in Tring High Street. In the background the timbered building is No.8 High Street – 'Oasis'. The white building, one of the oldest in Tring, is now a restaurant. Where these shelters stood is now the car park and site of the Friday market.

Filling sandbags outside the Market House in Akeman Street. On the left is Mr Bull, the foreman, next to him is George Turner. The man holding the sack is 'Happy' Adams. The young man above him is Harry 'Splash' Kempster and the other young man on the bags, with the waistcoat, is Joe Kempster. The man bending over is 'Knock' Eggleton and the boy on the bags to the right is Harry Mills.

Tring ARP rescue section photographed outside the stable block at Tring Park. Back row: Maurice Bradding, Bill Jones, Bert Archer, Don Cartwright, -?-, Nat Gower, Bill Budd, Fred Cox, Mr Nutkins. Middle row: Bill Lovell, Fred Copcutt, Ted Bagnall, Fred Jakeman, Harry Bull, Jimmy Attryde, Fred Nutkins, -?-, Benjamin Gower. Front row: Bert Potter, George Copcutt, Arthur 'Junky' Baldwin, Joe Kempster, Tom Grace, Arnold Halsey, Charles Ginger, Wally Rance, Tom Moy, G. Bradding.

Tring ARP. Back row: -?-, Bob Hedges, -?-, -?-, -?-, -?-, Fred Hurdle, Sid Horne, Mr Desborough, -?-, -?-, -?-. Third row: John Bingham, Edgar Bagnall, -?-, Mr Gibbs, Jim Finney, Cyril Howlett, Ernest Clark, -?-, -?-, -?-, -?-, Mr Higgs, Albert Spencer, Ernest Childs, -?-, -?-. Second row: -?-, -?-, -?-, -?-, -?-, Hubert G. Gurney, -?-, Mr Vranch, -?-, Harry Bull, Jack Hummerston, -?-, -?-, Miss Pearsall, Delia Henderson. Front row: Les Parslow, -?-, Mr Kenyon-Bell, Sid Luck, Edward Bell, Sid Rance, -?-, -?-, -?-, Frank Rance, George Rance, -?-, Mr Bradding.

A parade of civilian volunteers in Western Road in 1939. In the uniformed group on the front are Reg Sallery, 'Choice' Higby, Tom Fulks and Leon Baker. Either side of Reg are Fred Fleckney and Will Higby. The group on the left side include Mary Kemp, with son Roy, in the pram; Alice Church with son Bob; Mr Harry Kempster and Mrs Kempster with son Joe.

Part of the 1939 parade of volunteers along the Western Road. These are the Air Raid Wardens with Mr Vranch (of Cash & Co.) in front, the man on the left of that front group is Freddy Hurdle (manager of the post office).

Men of the Auxiliary Fire Service lead civilian volunteers in the parade along Western Road.

More volunteers in Western Road.

Local children also became involved with the war effort, here we see Tring school boys digging ARP trenches for the school in the meadow next to the playground.

The children of New Mill can be seen selling their sacks of herbs to the collector. Herb gathering was essential during the war as herbs for medicines could not be imported as they had been. The children were only paid a few pence per pound but, with the exception of nettles, picking herbs was not an unpleasant job and the children could feel they were helping the war effort. This photograph, taken in July 1944, shows Meads flour mills in the background.

Tring Home Guard, 7C (18) Company, Platoon No. 3, photographed in front of Tring Mansion. Back row: Frank Kent, Fred Edwards, -?-, Frank List, Derek Petty, -?-. Fourth row: -?-, -?-, Wyndham Budd, Len 'Sassa' Wright, Reg Potter, -?-, Bob Kempster, -?-, -?-. Third row: Mr Cook, ? Bell, Len Wren, -?-, Les Goodson, Tommy Blackburn, -?-, Ivan Wright, 'Tich' Routley. Second row: -?-, -?-, B. Kemp, Don Roberts, -?-, Bert Allen, -?-, -?-, -?-, -?-. First row: -?-, Joe Budd, Albert Clarkson, Sgt Bowers, Lt Hobbs, Capt. Lovering, -?-, -?-, -?-, -?-, -?-. Front: Fred Gray, Stan Hall, Percy Hart, 'Bek' Jakeman, -?-, -?-, -?-, G. Rance.

HMS *Aeolus*. (Aeolus: Greek God of the Winds). This picture of the staff of HMS *Aeolus* was taken in the grounds of Tring Mansion. The depot was at 51-52 High Street, Tring, where Metcalfe's hardware shop is today. They supplied kites and balloons to dockyards in the UK and abroad. These were transferred to ships, mainly merchant shipping, who flew them to combat low flying attacking aircraft. The balloons were like small barrage balloons and the kites were made of canvas with bamboo struts. Back row: Eric Cox, Phil Watts, -?-, -?-, Len Bull, -?-, -?-, Doug Hughes, -?-, Mr Brackett, -?-, -?-, -?-, Jim Fowler. Middle row: -?-, Mr Rance, Charlie Finch, Nancy Nutkins, Phyllis Gates, -?-, Arthur Church, George Reynolds, -?-, -?-, -?-, -?-, -?- , Joy Rance, Les Doughty, Phyllis Nutkins. Front row, sitting: -?-, -?-, -?-, -?-, Miss Scott (secretary), -?-, Lt. Commander Hamer (paymaster), Cmdr Boorman, Lt. Danson, -?-, Mr Russell (civilian manager), Vera Gurney, -?-, Audrey Mansfield, -?-.

Volunteer, retained and AFS at the end of the war in 1945. Back row: J. Dwight, Mr Wright, -?-, E. Rolfe, Frank Smith, E. Higby, Harry Saunders, Leon Baker, Eddie Brackley, C. Gregory. Third row: Mr Robinson, F. Whittle, Ron Hicks, S. Stevens, Mr Dumpleton, J. Wood, Arthur Higby, Mr Burch, -?-, Arthur Flitney, Archie Fulks, A. West. Second row: Fred Chandler, R. Cousins, William Barber, H. Cutler, Mr Gregory, Dick Green, Bert Nutkins, Mr Sear, Tom Fulks, Ray Pheasant, Mr Kennedy, Mr Wander, George Hinton, M. Foster. Front row: Jock Wilson, Mary Luck, Miss Warburton, Kathy Gower, Jack Lines, Reg Sallery, Mr Burton, George Goodliffe, Harry Bull, H. Harrop, E. Haddon, ? Hart.

The National Savings chart on the wall of Wheeler Brothers' shop in the High Street. Wheeler Bros. was the chief selling centre for National Saving Certificates during 'Salute the Soldier Week'. During this week alone, having previously raised nearly £750,000, Tring raised a further £121,564. This represented £24 per head of the population, a large sum in 1944. Painting in the Spitfire is Harry Fennimore from Bushell Bros.

Ten

Public Houses and Inns

The Green Man, No.5 Lower High Street. John Philby brewed here in 1846 but by 1851 the inn keeper was Jane Philbey, a widow. Also at the inn was Jane's nephew, twelve-year-old John Meager, who was the publican in 1870. John Woodman kept the inn from 1878 to 1895. He was a widower and was assisted by his daughters, Mary and Kate. The inn was used by many local societies for their annual dinners; the Tring Association dinner in 1887 cost £4 for twenty people. The Green Man was pulled down by Lord Rothschild in 1895.

The old Rose and Crown, around the turn of the century. It was an old coaching inn and stood level with the other buildings until it was demolished by the Rothschilds around 1905. In the 1851 census Sarah Northwood was the inn keeper with six living-in staff. In the 1890s the hotel keeper was Jabez Thorn assisted by his wife, Caroline, their son Jesse, and their daughter-in-law Annie. The building on the left of the photograph is the gatehouse of Tring Mansion and contained a mechanism for opening and closing the large ornamental gates.

The hotel photographed after it had been rebuilt by the Rothschild Estate 1905-06. It was built to William Huckvale's design and on its completion was made over to the Hertfordshire Public House Trust, forerunner of Trust House Forte. It continued to be used by visitors to the mansion, including Prince Edward, the Prince of Wales, in 1935. The shop on the right hand side was for many years De Fraines, stationers, newsagents and booksellers, and was the branch office of the *Bucks Herald*.

The Robin Hood in Brook Street around the turn of the century, next door to William Bly's furniture shop. It was a seventeenth century building but much altered and restored. In 1806 the landlord was William Tapping and in the 1850s it was Ann Tompkins; by 1870 Henry Becket was in charge. The 1891 census lists the licensed victualler as Charles Harrison, assisted by his wife Sarah. They obtained their supplies from Roberts & Wilson of Ivinghoe.

This is one of the oldest surviving public houses in Tring. In 1611 Henry Geary was before the Justices for keeping the Bell without a licence and a few years later for drunkenness. In the 1660s tokens were issued by Hastings Parrot of the Bell, as small change was in short supply. Some of these rare coins still exist, also those of other tradesmen in the town. In the 1870s and, 80s Joseph Norris was the publican, later in the century John Evans, followed by David Hart, and in the first two decades of the this century Edgar Short was in residence.

The original George Hotel in Frogmore Street was described as a small hostelry and corn chandlers held in 1806 by Joseph Tompkins and by William Clark in 1830. It was rebuilt and enlarged to reach the High Street at the end of the nineteenth century by the Aylesbury Brewery Company. The building was more recently used by John Hervery, a mail order clothing business, and is now an estate agent.

The Britannia, Western Road, was built by John Brown of Tring Brewery in the 1840s, chiefly to cater for the navvies working on the London to Birmingham Railway. In 1870 the publican was Charles Smith and in the 1890s Job Archer was there with his wife, Rebecca. The Britannia is now a private home renamed Norfolk House.

The Anchor, Western Road in the early 1970s. It is still a pub and looks much the some today. Built in the last century it was then a beerhouse and in 1891 was kept by Alfred Barber and his wife, Jane; at the turn of the century William Wells was in charge. Kellys directory of 1933 lists Samuel Nightingale Jnr. beer retailer at 25 Western Road.

The Castle in Park Road was built in the last century and still enjoys a clear view of the downs. The photograph was taken in the late 1960s and the public house has altered little over the years. In 1870 the publican was William Loyd and he was there with his wife, Harriet, until the 1890s. In 1899 the landlord was George Robert Ives and in 1933-37 it was Ephraim Hearn.

The Swan, Akeman Street in the 1930s. It was a popular pub in Victorian times and was frequented by many of the mansion staff and known locally as the 'butlers' pub. In the 1880s Joseph Gurney lived there with his wife, Mary Ann. Some later publicans have been George Murrey, Thomas Scott, Charles Humphreys, Hy Ives, and Tom Saunders. The Swan is now a private house.

Wingrave Road, New Mill. On the right is the Queens Arms public house. In 1891 the publican was thirty-year-old Frederick Philby, who lived there with his wife, Annie, and their one-year-old son, also named Frederick. The Queens Arms, known to locals as 'Red House' closed on 24 February 1974. The council bought the land, demolished the pub and built new houses, calling the road Elizabeth Drive to commemorate the Queen's Silver Jubilee.

Eleven

Nearby Places

An early photograph of Aldbury, one of Hertfordshire's most picturesque villages, which nestles at the foot of rising beechwoods that form part of Ashridge Park, now owned by the National Trust. The magnificent elm tree by the pond, featured for so many years in postcards and photographs, has sadly now gone, the victim of Dutch elm disease.

A view of Aldbury in around 1910, taken from the church tower. The pond can just be seen on the left, and the Memorial Hall on the right. The church of St John the Baptist is partly thirteenth century, or earlier, and has a flint-faced tower. The village still has a lot of its sixteenth- and seventeenth-century, timber-framed, brick and tile cottages and, although more modern houses have been added, it still retains its old-world charm.

The word 'Aldbury' means old fort in Anglo Saxon and the village was already settled in pre-Saxon times. This photograph, probably taken in the 1930s, shows The Greyhound in the centre. In the 1891 census we see the publican was Rachel Long, a sixty-one-year-old widow. The house to the left was the old post office, and last century it was run by John Dolt and his niece Eliza M. Glenister. On the right one can just see Town Farm where the farm buildings have now been converted into dwellings and the house does mouth watering cream teas.

Pitstone. It is said that Pitstone was first settled in the Iron Age, and a mammoth tooth, recovered locally, is in the Pitstone Museum. As with other villages, the nearby Icknield Way to East Anglia encouraged settlement. It was once dominated by the Pitstone Cement Works which has now closed. Although part of the area has become a nature reserve, conservationists are now trying to prevent the rest from becoming a huge waste dump. When Samuel Hawkins came to Pitstone in 1808 he started a line of Hawkins farmers at Pitstone Green Farm that has extended to the present day. The farm, today run by Mr Jeff Hawkins, houses the Pitstone Museum.

Church End, Pitstone, early this century. These 'two up, two down' cottages housed mainly labourers and their families. The 1891 census records Reuben Wilkins living in one of these small dwellings with his wife and seven children.

The first reference to the Manor of Marsworth was made in the year 970, when Elgive, sister-in-law to Edgar, King of Wessex, wrote that she would leave him in her will the Manor of Marsworth, as well as Wing, Linslade and Haversham. In the Domesday book Marsworth or Missworde as it was written then, was held by Ralph Bassett. In 1739 one third part was sold to William Gore of Tring Park. The remaining portions were later sold to the Bridgewater family and were the property of the Earl Brownlow. The records of All Saints church go back to the sixteenth century although extensive repairs were carried out in the 1800s.

The White Lion, Marsworth. A popular pub on the Grand Union Canal. The 1891 census records that Elizabeth Jellis, a forty-two-year-old widow, was there with her nineteen-year-old son William.

Long Marston in 1903. The shop and cottage beyond are now a pair of private houses. The cottages in the distance are much the same today, but the space between now has a house and the village hall built in it.

Long Marston showing the Station Road-Cheddington Road corner. The gentleman sitting by the front gate is Mr John Chappin. Down the Cheddington Road can be seen the Long Marston Baptist Chapel which was erected in 1869. This view has altered little since this photograph was taken.

Wilstone early this century. On the right is the Buckingham Arms, run in 1891 by William Cartwright, living there with his wife and their five children. This is now two private dwellings, though the names still include the word 'Buckingham'. Almost hidden between cottages further down is Wilstone's surviving public house, 'The Half Moon'. The publican in 1891 was James Reeve with his wife Elizabeth and their large family of five daughters and three sons. From 1906 Walter Cartwright was the landlord and, when he was killed in France in 1918, his wife Lavinia was the landlady until her retirement in 1936.

Wilstone showing Long Row on the left hand side with Mrs Denchfield's shop on the corner which is now a private house. The old cottages on the right hand side have since been demolished.

Gubblecote, called Bublecote in the Domesday book, was described as part of the land the Count of Mortain had taken from Tring. This old cottage, at Gubblecote Cross, stands near the place where local records say that Tring chimney-sweep, Thomas Colley, was hanged for the murder of an old lady, Ruth Osbourne, on 24 August 1745. She and her husband were accused of witchcraft and a mob tried to drown them in Long Marston pond. Only Mrs Osbourne died and Colley was accused as a ringleader. The persecution of witches had officially ceased in 1736.

Drayton Beauchamp. Early in the thirteenth century William de Beauchamp held the Manor of Drayton, and although the family only stayed for two generations they gave their name to the village of Drayton Beauchamp. A church was first mentioned in the eleventh century, but the present church dates from the fifteenth century, although the Norman font dates from the twelfth. Baptisms were first registered in 1538, burials in 1567 and marriages in 1541.

There was a settlement on the site of Buckland Village centuries before the Normans came, as it had an important position near the Lower Icknield Way, a road dating back to pre-Roman times. It is mentioned in the Domesday Book and has had a series of Lords of the Manor. The church was built in the thirteenth century. It fell into disrepair and might have been lost had it not been taken over by the wealthy, if rather eccentric, Revd Edward Bonus in the nineteenth century. Buckland Common, once part of the parish of Buckland, was, in the 1930s, joined with Cholesbury and Hawridge.

Puttenham, although now a tiny hamlet, was once much larger, the church being the centre of the village with a rector and manor house. The name is derived from the de Puttenhams, the family who occupied the manor for five generations before Queen Elizabeth I came to the throne. The church was first mentioned in the twelfth century, and the fifteenth century tower is one of only two in Hertfordshire with chequer-work formed by limestone and flints. Many local people still remember services and weddings being held by candlelight in the church, as electricity was not installed until 1975.

The early days of flying at Halton. The Rothschild Estate at Halton was first used by the army for manoeuvres in 1913. When the war started Lord Rothschild offered the use of the estate to the army and the Royal Flying Corps came in 1916 and the camp was used for training recruits. In 1917 the army left, though a unit of the Australian Flying Corps joined the RFC that year. In 1918 the Air Ministry took over Halton House and it became the Officers Mess. An aircraft Apprentice scheme started in 1919 and the RAF have been training young airman there to this day.

In the Domesday book Halton was described as the lands of Lanfranc, Archbishop of Canterbury. In 1853 the manor and estate of Halton were purchased by Lionel de Rothschild, but it was not until the 1880s that his son, Alfred, built Halton House in what was called the 'free French Chateau style'. The church of St Michael, although old in origin, was entirely rebuilt in 1813, the work paid for by Sir J.D. King, then patron and Lord of the Manor.

'Aston' meant 'East-Town and 'Clinton' was added as the name of the early owners. In 113?
the manor was in the hands of William de Clinton. Centuries later Sir Anthony de Rothschild
built himself Aston Clinton House, a manor later demolished except for the stable block. This
view, taken around 1918, shows the London Road photographed from the Weston Turville
turn. In the middle we can see W. Gates general store, later to become Cooks Store.

St Leonards was described in a survey of 1861 as a 'scattered hamlet' included in the parish of
Aston Clinton. There are records of a church in the thirteenth century, largely rebuilt after the
Civil War. It fell into disrepair and was restored and decorated in 1845-6. One of the oldest
buildings in the village, Dundridge Cottage, seen here in the last century, has been
sympathetically restored by its present owners.

Wigginton High Street, showing The Brewhouse public house. In 1891 Jane Baker, a seventy-seven-year-old widow, was the 'beerhouse keeper'. It is now a private residence, restored to retain the original character.

Hawridge and Cholesbury mill is situated just off Cholesbury common, on the road known as Rays Hill, and the first records of it were in 1863. It was then made of wood but when this fell into disrepair in the 1880s it was remade in stone. A cottage was added at the base of the tower and used as a grain store. Used as a mill until the First World War, it was then converted into a private dwelling and lived in until the Second World War. It was then neglected, lost its sails and was almost derelict until it was purchased and restored in the late 1960s. Still a family home today, the mill is a dominant feature in the Cholesbury countryside.

Tring Ford around 1920 with the farm in the background, now called Piggeries Pine. Tring Ford reservoir was built when the Wendover branch canal was opened and is said to be 405 feet above sea level, a trifle higher than the summit of St Paul's Cathedral.

Cooks Wharf near the Grand Union canal on the road to Cheddington. The Duke of Wellington public house is still there today. In 1891 the publican was thirty-two-year-old William Turvey, who lived with his wife, Eliza, and their two daughters, Ada and Ellen, aged six and four.

IMAGES
of England

AROUND
TRING
THE SECOND SELECTION

Compiled by
Mike Bass and Jill Fowler

TEMPUS

The circus parade passes the Bell Inn in the High Street around the turn of the century. The circus came regularly to Tring and it was an exciting day for the children who were given the day off school. A report of 1887 says that Lord John Sanger and Son's circus, menagerie, museum and hippodrome visited Tring and gave two performances in the Green Man Meadow, now the site of the Friday market. By 1898 it was described as George Sanger's circus.

Contents

A very old photograph of Tring Church, possibly taken in the 1860s, before the restoration of the 1880s.

Introduction

When we had finished the first *Around Tring* book we felt that we had given quite a comprehensive view of the life and times of the town in the hundred years up to the 1970s. The book aroused widespread interest, with many people discovering family and friends in the photographs, or places where they had lived or worked. Others felt that they had material that would have been just as interesting if they had known that the book was being produced and have generously made it available to us now. This Second Selection of entirely different photographs includes a few of the same subjects but there are several new ones. Many newcomers to the town live in a group of modern homes where there once stood a grand house and its grounds, inhabited by an influential family. We have tried to show some of these grand houses as they were in the early days. Some of the houses still stand, though most are no longer family homes, but the names of others have been preserved in the road names.

Pendley Manor and the Williams family have always been rather overshadowed in local history by Tring Mansion and the Rothschilds, so we have attempted to tell briefly the story of Pendley in one chapter.

Farming always plays an important part in the life of a country town. Old photographs show that methods have changed a lot over the years and sadly many farms have now gone and horses now graze many of the fields that once supported cattle or sheep. Tring is still surrounded by farmland though very few of the town's inhabitants are still employed in the industry, as they were a hundred years ago.

Researching this book has been fascinating and it is a constant source of wonder to meet Tring residents who can remember events and people often after more than seventy years. We are very grateful to them all. As comparative 'newcomers', only having lived in Tring since the early 1950s, we know we still have a lot to learn and are always pleased to hear from anyone who can give us advice or information. We can be contacted at 19/20 Charles Street, Tring, HP23 6BD.

We hope that this second selection of Tring photographs will revive memories for those born in the town and also prove interesting to those newcomers who have decided to make Tring their home.

The decorative entrance to the stable block at Pendley Manor. The outside of the stables has been sympathetically preserved by the Grass Roots Group, who took over the building several years ago, and they have adapted the area to house a modern company. More of the Pendley Estate and its history can be seen in Chapter Three.

Acknowledgements

Iris Anderson, Wendy Austin, The Automobile Association, John Bly, Mervyn Bone, John Bowman, John and Jennie Branston, Connie Carter, Peter Cherry, B. Clarkson, Pam Cockerill, Len and Maureen Cousens, Murray Fieldhouse, First Tring Scout Group, June Fortune, Mary Fuller, Bob Grace, Gilbert and Julie Grace, Nora Grace, Pat Gower, Dennis and Erica Guy, Jeff Hawkins, Bill Hearn, Stephen Hearn, Hertfordshire County Record Office, Dulcie Hopcroft, Hunting Aerofilms Ltd Ref. A 48775 page 23, Keith Impey, Richard Johnson, Josie Jordan, Harold Kindell, Maurice Lacey, Frank Lockhart, Cecilia Menday, Muriel Orton, Pendley Manor Hotel, Rosemary Prentice, Gus Proctor, Miriam Ralph, Roland and Gladys Rance, Derek Reed, Don Reed, David Ridgwell, Doug Sinclair, Peggy Slemeck, Arthur Starling, Steve Southworth, Sue and Robert of Brightwood, Eirlys Thomas, Tring and District Local History and Museum Society, Jennifer Williams, Piers Williams, Ted and Marjorie Wright.

One
Around the Town

This painting of the Rose and Crown was made into a postcard that was posted on 17 April 1907. As the hotel was only opened the year before, this could have been based on the architect's design. It is interesting to note that although the Rose and Crown faces due north it appears here to be in full sunshine. In its prominent position opposite the parish church, it is still popular with visitors to the town today.

Tring High Street in the early nineteenth century from a painting believed to be by Brussadet.
The building with the large doorway is the old Rose and Crown. Later this and the two shops
beyond were demolished to be replaced by the new hotel in 1905-6. In the distance can be seen
the sign of the Bell public house and on the right that of the Plough Inn, now an antique shop.
The buildings this side of the Rose and Crown still exist, though their appearance has been
greatly altered by the Rothschilds. Those beyond were replaced in the mid-nineteenth century
by the ones there today.

This picture of the High Street taken in 1893, from a similar perspective to that of the painting,
shows that the artist was most observant in his view of the town. The building just on the left
of the picture is the shop of E.C. Bird, printers, engravers and stationers. The signs of the two
public houses can be seen here, one in the centre and the other on the right.

Market day in the Lower High Street in 1897, with decorations for the visit of the Prince of Wales, later Edward VII. The picture below shows another market there in the 1930s, demonstrating how little the area has altered in the intervening years. It was not until forty years later that the Friday market moved to the car park, built on the field behind the wall, where it is now held.

THOMAS BAILEY & SON,
FAMILY GROCERS AND TEA DEALERS,
HIGH STREET, TRING.
Superior British Wines.   Home Cured Hams and Bacon.

This elaborate design was originally printed in full colour. In the 1851 census Thomas Bailey was a grocer at No. 53 High Street and was aged 51. Susan his wife, the same age, was a straw bonnet maker and they had three children at home still unmarried, Elizabeth aged twenty-five, Lucy aged twenty-two and Thomas aged seventeen. Lucy was also a straw bonnet maker and young Thomas worked with his father. Records show that the Baileys were still there in 1865 but by the 1880s the shop, still a grocer's, was run by John Putman. The picture would not appear to have any connection with the grocer's, though William Goodson, the blacksmith, had premises about two doors away. No. 53 is now Harmony of Tring, selling health foods.

The High Street in the 1930s, with the garage of Robins and Marriott on the right. In 1899 William James and Arthur Henry Dawe were ironmongers and cycle agents here and continued for many years. In the early 1930s Robins and Marriott had the garage and carried on until the late 1930s. After the war the premises were purchased by Mr Bob Metcalfe who opened an ironmonger's and household and garden supplies business in October of that year. Metcalfe's is still one of Tring's most popular shops and celebrated its fiftieth anniversary in 1998.

The High Street in the 1930s with passengers just boarding the Aldbury bus. The Rose and Crown and the shops beyond it look much the same today. On the right is the ivy-covered wall of the building that was William Brown and Co., land agents, architects and surveyors. The name has been retained to this day as it is now Brown and Merry, the estate agents.

The High Street in the early 1930s. De Fraine's shop on the left was a prominent business in Tring for many years, as a stationer's and bookseller's, and it was also the *Bucks Herald* office. The unusual doorway has not been altered and now forms the entrance to an estate agent's.

Tring High Street, looking west towards the crossroads, in 1897. This was the year of Queen Victoria's Diamond Jubilee and the town was decorated for the visit of the Prince of Wales, later Edward VII. On the Akeman Street corner can be seen the house of Mr Mead, the butcher, where the Market House now stands. The little building on the opposite side is the same today and is at present a sandwich bar. On the right of the picture is Greening's, tailors and clothiers, run then by Richard Greening. It was still in the family in the 1930s when William Greening was in charge. It now houses the Woolwich bank and building society.

The crossroads in the first decade of the twentieth century. This part of the High Street looks much the same today, though the school in the distance has now gone and the fence on the left shows where the police station is yet to be built.

14

A circus rider coming through the town around 1900, watched by the local children. The house in the background is the home of Mr Mead, the butcher, and a few years later the new Market House replaced it. It was very rare to see a successful action photograph taken with the photographic equipment at the time but Frank Grace, who took this, was a very experienced photographer and managed to adjust the shutter on his camera to produce such an effective picture of this horse and rider.

This postcard, sent in June 1924, shows that Tring High Street has not altered much over the following seventy years. The policeman would not be seen standing on the corner of Akeman Street these days and the two young men would not be able to lean on their bicycles chatting, with the endless traffic that still comes through Tring in spite of the bypass opened in the 1970s. The George ceased to be a hotel several years ago and is now an estate agent's.

Frogmore Street, c. 1915. In 1890 Charles Griffin had a grocer's and tea merchant's business at No. 38, on the left of this postcard. In the 1930s it was run by Mr George Goodliffe. Just beyond the group of people is the Dolphin Inn. Known as the Dolphin Beerhouse, it was purchased by the Reverend Arthur Frederick Pope and converted to a Workmen's Hall. Now part of Tring's shopping precinct, the old inn gave its name to what is now Dolphin Square.

16

Two views of the upper part of Frogmore Street in the early 1970s. Most of these buildings were swept away when the Dolphin Square shopping precinct was built. The shop seen just on the right of the top photograph was a DIY store run by Mr Arthur Starling who still has a shoe shop in the same premises.

An old part of the town seen from the church tower. Church Lane runs down the left side of the photograph from Frogmore Street to the church. This area was cleared when Budgen's and Dolphin Square were built.

Looking up Church Lane in the 1960s. The side entrance to the church can just be seen in the distance.

Tring High Street, c. 1915. The police station has now been built beyond the New Market House on the left. Horses were still the more usual mode of transport, but a motor car coming through the town would not cause the attention and astonishment that one had done little more than fifteen years before.

WE'RE DOING OUR DUTY

High Street

FOR KING AND COUNTRY AT TRING

During the First World War earlier photographs were reprinted to produce a series of patriotic postcards from Tring. This one shows the Conservative clubrooms on the left, with Grace and Son's shop beyond, and the post office on the right.

A very early photograph taken in Akeman Street, showing the Harrow public house, now demolished. Beyond it can be seen the railings and gateway of the Baptist chapel. On the right of the picture is Grace's Malting, now a private house, and on the left the little shop was Grace's bakery, later Warrior's, also a bakery. It is now a shop selling individual children's clothes and called 'Sticky Fingers'.

Surrey Place, Akeman Street, in May 1965, seen from a window in the Tring Museum. In 1891 there were nine cottages here, housing forty-seven people. By 1965 there was only one still occupied, the Baldwin family living at No. 6. Here most of the houses are derelict and due for demolition. A complex of retirement flats has been built in the area, still called Surrey Place. In the earlier aerial photograph, on the next page, the houses can be seen in the lower centre overlooked on two sides by the museum. They were occupied at that time and the gardens tended.

An aerial photograph from the early 1960s.

Here the old cottages in Surrey Place have gone and the new homes are yet to be built. The entrance to Albert Street can be seen across Akeman Street. The old shops and cottage on the right side of Albert Street were due for demolition so that the William Batey electronic business could expand their premises.

Park Street towards the end of the nineteenth century before the Louisa Cottages were extended in 1901. This atmospheric picture was taken by Aylesbury photographers Mr and Mrs S.G. Payne and Son, who also had a Tring branch in Albert Street. The museum on the right is now surrounded by a low wall and the little yew bush has become a tree obscuring part of the view which is otherwise very much the same today.

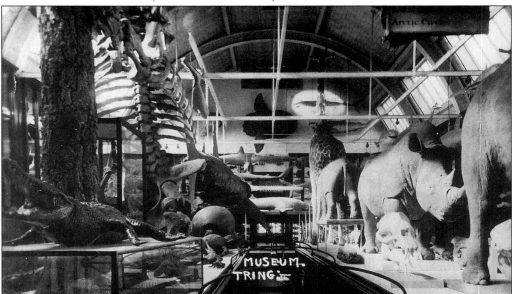

The museum in the 1930s. Tring has been famous for its Natural History Museum since it was formed by Walter Rothschild who sent collectors all over the world to obtain specimens for him. It was opened to the public in 1892 and is still attracting thousands of visitors a year.

An early photograph showing the Park Street entrance to Tring Mansion. The big house on the left is one of the oldest buildings in Tring. Sir Nicholas Pevsner (1902-1983), the German-born British art historian who produced a huge series of Penguin books entitled *The Buildings of England*, noted that the only building in Tring worth mentioning was this Queen Anne house.

An aerial view of Tring taken in April 1953, showing Tring mansion in the foreground. The tall square building in the upper centre is the Baptist church in Akeman Street and further across on the edge of the town is the Regal cinema, now the site of Regal Court, with the Church House next to it. There was very little development on the northern side of the town when this photograph was taken.

This picture was taken soon after Messrs J. Honour and Sons built the first part of the Louisa Cottages in 1893, from designs by Mr W. Huckvale. The photographer was standing in the grounds of Prospect House School opposite. The school and grounds were sold to Lord Rothschild at the end of the previous year for £5,000 by the executors of the late Mr Mark Young, who had been headmaster for nearly fifty years. The school did continue for some time on this site before moving to Brook Street when Lord Rothschild demolished the buildings to clear the land.

The almshouses and museum around 1902, showing the sharp bend that has caused numerous accidents in the past. Only recently one of the almshouses was badly damaged by a car that failed to slow down enough to turn the corner. In the 1890s there was a report of a horse and carriage hitting the corner and then rebounding on to the museum railings, overturning the carriage and throwing out the two occupants, who suffered quite severe injuries.

24

The eastern end of King Street, a part of Tring rarely photographed, although Cyril Alfred Howlett, a well known Tring photographer, ran the Post Office and Stores just seen on the left, on the corner with Queen Street. Although taken in the 1950s, this picture would look strange to today's residents as there are now cars parked on both sides of the road. Fortunately this part of King Street is wider than most of the other streets of Victorian cottages in the area. The Roman Catholic Corpus Christi church and bungalow can be seen in Langdon Street at the far end.

Western Road seen from the Miswell Lane – Chapel Street crossroads before 1920. Most of the buildings on the left were private homes; now all are used for commercial purposes, although the first three tall houses have been altered very little. Beyond them shop fronts have been fitted and the businesses include shoe repairs, a bakery and a newsagent. The shop with the blind is now a Chinese takeaway. The cycle shop almost at the end of the row was founded by Mr Benjamin Kingham at the end of the nineteenth century and bicycles were sold and repaired there until 1971, all the time remaining the same family business.

Two of the town's newer roads, Drummond Ride and Nathaniel Walk, in January 1962. Both the road names have a connection with Tring Park. Sir Drummond Smith was the owner of the estate until his death and it was sold to William Kay in 1823. The first Lord Rothschild was named Nathaniel and as he had a hunting lodge in Dundale beyond the trees on the left of the lower photograph, he could have walked there from the Mansion.

Duckmore Lane, from a window of the West Leith cottage 'Glenmullen' in the winter of 1945-6. The houses in the Aylesbury Road can just be seen in the distance and the allotments between are still being cultivated. The lane to the right goes up to West Leith Farm, Stubbins Wood and the Holloway. On several occasions in severe weather this narrow lane would be completely blocked with snow and a tractor from the farm would tow vehicles up through the adjoining field.

Rose Cottage used to stand almost at the end of the Lower High Street, opposite the Co-operative Stores and Unity Hall. In 1851 it housed the Faithfull family: thirty-year-old Mary with a four-year-old daughter also called Mary, a nursemaid, Elizabeth Pessell, and a servant, Sarah Stevens.

The cattle market in Brook Street in the 1930s. This was purpose-built, complete with an office building, by Lord Rothschild early in the twentieth century. Before that, the market had been held in the Lower High Street, previously known as Market Street.

New Mill Terrace in the late 1920s. The house with the sunblind was No. 20; Alice Wilkins had a shop there and was licensed to sell tobacco and snuff.

Moving further down the same road at New Mill, c. 1912. The second three-storey house on the right was a beerhouse known as the White Hart and the name can still faintly be seen painted on the brickwork. The Pheasant public house, now known as The New Mill, can be seen in the distance.

Further on still, approaching the crossroads where the Bulbourne and Dunstable road turns right in front of the Gamnel Road School, also around 1912. On the left is the Queens Arms public house, which was pulled down in the 1970s, when Elizabeth Drive was built there. Mead's Flour Mill, now Heygates, the Grand Union Canal and the Tring Reservoirs are further along the road which leads straight ahead.

Tring Reservoirs, c. 1918. The reservoirs were dug to top up the water in the canal network as the hilly countryside resulted in the need for numerous locks. This area is still beautiful and popular with local walkers and bird watchers. Although the reservoirs are thought of locally as 'nature reserves', Lord Rothschild still holds the gaming, hunting and fishing rights over them and there are still duck shoots several times a year.

This little boy is sitting on the bridge at Tring Reservoirs around 1910. With the recent dry summers this overflow is not often seen with water flowing over it.

Two
Shops and Businesses

William Bly, furniture dealer and broker, was listed at No. 11 Akeman Street in 1890. He was the brother of John Bly who had his shop in the High Street. Before the end of the century, William had moved to Nos 2, 3 and 4 Brook Street, shown here. He ran the shop until the 1930s when it was taken over by his son Frederick Stanley, always known as Bob. An antique shop for many more years, it is now the premises of David Doyle the estate agent.

John and Sarah Ann Gower stand in the entrance to their general store at Nos 56 and 57 High Street. In the other doorway is their son Benjamin Saunders Gower and the little boy is thought to be Bert Johnson. John and Sarah had a big family and the shop was later run by Archie and Nathaniel, their oldest and youngest sons, and finally by Philip and Peter Gower, Nathaniel's two sons. Below is a much more recent photograph, taken in the 1950s; the shop has not been altered much. It was later bought by singer Dennis Lotis, who ran a restaurant there with his wife Rena. Afterwards it was another restaurant, 'Trattoria Pinnocchio', before being left empty for some time. It is now the premises of Secureglaze, a double glazing firm.

A very early photograph of three High Street shops. In the 1882 Kelly's directory No. 10 was occupied by Mrs Mary Prouse, a saddler and harness maker, no. 11 by Frederick Marsh, a chemist, and No. 12 by James Jones, a grocer. These shops still stand but have been 'cladded' by the Rothschilds to look as they do now. Just beyond is the entrance to Tring Park and on the far left the tall building is E.C. Bird, printers and stationers.

Numbers 14, 15 and 16 High Street with part of the old Rose and Crown just seen on the left. Jesse Wright, the butcher, is pictured with his sons Will and Frank. The next shop is that of Henry Stevens, a boot and shoe maker who later moved to Chesham and founded a boot factory there. Number 16 was the premises of Edward Craddock Knight. In the 1890s the Kelly's Directory described Mr Knight as a 'decorator, gas fitter and plumber, painter, house painter and stationer'. When the old Rose and Crown was demolished around 1905 these three shops suffered the same fate to make way for the considerably larger hotel.

Grace's ironmongers shop at No. 34 in the High Street. The business was established in 1750, trading in Frogmore Street, then moved to a shop next to the old Market House, in front of the church. In the early nineteenth century Charles Grace lived and traded at No. 29 Akeman Street. Kelly's Directory lists Grace's as being at No. 34 High Street in 1890, but by June 1891 Mr Gilbert Grace had built a new shop and house opposite the old post office, where the business is still being run by the present Mr Gilbert Grace.

Mr Harry Johnson in the doorway of his fish shop in the 1880s. Next to it can be seen part of the old Market House in front of the church. The shop and the Market House were demolished in 1900 when the area was cleared. By 1891 Johnson's had moved across the High Street to No. 22 and then they finally opened their shop in Frogmore Street on the corner of Parsonage Place.

34

John Bly's High Street antique business was founded towards the end of the nineteenth century. It stayed at No. 22, above, and for a short time at No. 21, until the premises were pulled down and the Midland Bank was built on the site. The business then moved to No. 50 where it remained until almost the end of the twentieth century when the shop became New England House Antiques. John Bly still has premises at the rear of No. 50 but has moved his main retail shop to London. The first John Bly, who started the business with his wife, Letitia, was succeeded by his son, Frank, whose son, John, later took over. John is well known as an expert in the antique field, he lectures in both Britain and America, and is frequently seen on television in programmes like the *Antiques Roadshow* and *Heirloom*. Standing in the doorway is little Frank with his older sister Doris.

The butcher's shop of the Mead brothers, Ernest and Walter, in Western Road, decorated for Christmas. Their father, John Mead, died in 1886, having drowned in the pond at Dundale. Mr Kempster is the young man standing in the doorway. The Meads' premises consisted of a shop, slaughterhouse and a private house on the corner of Akeman Street. Demolition of these started in 1898 to enable the New Market House to be built there, but the Meads had fine modern premises built nearby for them so that they could continue their business. Barclays Bank now occupies that site.

This photograph was taken before 1902 when the International Stores was still at No. 35 High Street, next to the entrance to the Bell's Yard. They then moved to what was then still called Western Road, now the upper part of the High Street, and the premises here were occupied by William James Green, who made, repaired and sold bicycles. Mr Harry Osborne is driving the donkey cart, known as the 'Wigginton Express'.

The International Stores in what was then Western Road, c. 1907, showing the staff of young men who were employed there at that time. Mr John Hedges and Sons, decorators and glaziers, formerly occupied the building, which was next to Grace's.

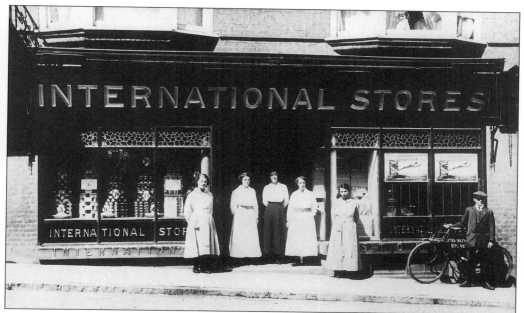

The International Stores during the First World War. This photograph taken in the same place less than ten years later shows a very similar pose but the staff are now all young ladies, with the exception of a young boy with his delivery bicycle. The men were away fighting for their country in the war.

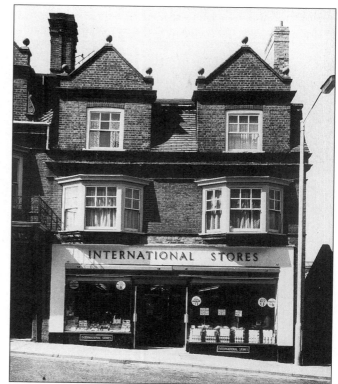

The International Stores in the 1960s. When the shop finally closed, the premises were taken over by Grace's next door, in order to enlarge their shop.

Evans the butchers at No. 55 High Street in the early part of the twentieth century. There had been a butcher's shop on these premises for many years. Records in 1851 show Augustus Seaton here with his wife and twenty-one-year-old son, also a butcher. Later in the century William Fulks had the business. He had a wife and five children and it is interesting to note that he had an eighteen-year-old boarder, Ernest G. Gregory, as a butcher's apprentice. There are now Gregory's butchers shops in New Mill and Long Marston. Older Tring people remember Samuel Singlehurst in the shop in the 1930s and it is now part of the Sunspar health and beauty centre.

A fire in Honour and Sons' building yard in Akeman Street. Horses stabled there were led to safety but sadly a dog died in the blaze. Horse-drawn fire engines came from Tring, Aylesbury and Berkhamsted but the water pressure was so low that the firemen were unable to quench the flames. Someone was sent to the Chiltern Water Company to instruct them to increase the pressure and eventually the fire was brought under control. This caused the local authorities to investigate ways of improving water supplies in case of fire. Over £200 was raised by public subscription to replace Mr Honour's tools lost in the fire.

Walter Wilkins with his milk cart. Always known as Wally, he was a well known figure in Tring. Records of 1937 described him as a 'cowkeeper' of Bulbourne Road, New Mill. When it ceased to be used, the Dacorum Heritage Trust acquired the milk float for posterity with the aim of restoring it to its original condition.

Bushell's Boatyard at New Mill with Mead's Flour Mills in the background. John Bushell was employed from around 1850 by Mead's to build and repair canal boats mainly to bring grain to the mill and take away the flour, usually to London. John's son, Joseph, developed the boatyard into a separate business from about 1875 and his sons, Charles and Joseph, took over in 1912. When they retired in 1952 the land was used to extend the flour mill.

Tring Hill Café, *c.* 1960. Now called the Crow's Nest, it enjoys a magnificent view across to Mentmore from the back. In the 1960s the Wilcox family ran it. Young Jimmy Wilcox kept a collection of wild animals there, including a lion, and he was also a keen aviator. At the time, he was the youngest person in the country to hold a pilot's licence. Some of the aerial photographs of Tring at that time were taken from a plane with Jimmy at the controls. The café is now a Beefeater Restaurant and a Travelodge has been built at the far side of the building.

The New Inn, Buckland Wharf, by the canal on the Tring to Aston Clinton road. When this photograph was taken the canal was navigable from Wendover and was built as a feeder for the locks at the canal's summit. Today it is not navigable until it reaches Little Tring as it became silted and was never wide enough for the larger craft. There are now hopes to reopen the six-and-a-half-mile Wendover arm to its original source. The New Inn is no longer a public house but the building has been preserved and it is used for commercial purposes.

Three
Pendley Manor and the Williams Family

The original Pendley Manor is mentioned in the Domesday Book. William the Conqueror confiscated it in 1066 and it had a succession of owners, including several generations of the Verney and Anderson families. The manor house in this painting is said to have been built by Sir Edmund Verney, standard bearer to King Charles II, in the seventeenth century. It was abandoned at the beginning of the nineteenth century by Sir Simon Harcourt who objected to the disturbance caused by the construction of the nearby canal and railway. It burned down in 1835.

James Williams and his wife Elizabeth. James purchased the Pendley Estate and started planning the building of the manor house. He had hoped to buy the Tring Park Estate but was unable to match the price paid by Lord Rothschild. The 1851 census shows James, then aged thirty-seven, and Elizabeth living at Tring Mansion, as it was being rented at the time by Elizabeth's uncle, Joseph Grout. She was born Elizabeth Grout and they called their son, only two months old in 1851, Joseph Grout Williams, and it was he who later finished the building of the house. James was a clergyman and also a magistrate.

The Revd James Williams, of Glevening Hall in Suffolk, bought the Manor of Pendley in July 1868. He planned the building of a new manor house but died in 1871 before it could be completed and it was finished by his son, Joseph. The design was to be that of an old Tudor manor house with 'more recent additions'. While waiting for the house to be completed Joseph lived at 'The Chequers', near Butlers Cross, now the country home of the Prime Minister. The family moved into their new home in 1877.

The drawing room at Pendley Manor in 1894. In the same year Hampton and Sons of Pall Mall, London, issued a beautifully illustrated catalogue with fifty designs for artistic interiors which showed that this comfortable room was typical of a drawing room in the larger houses of the day.

Staff at Pendley Manor, 19 September 1888. Back row: S. Butcher, John Clement (butler), F. Sturman, Henry Beer. Front row: Mrs Vock with 'Glen', Mary Anne Wells with 'Gip', Emma (?).

Meet of the stag hounds at Pendley Manor, April 1898. The stag hounds were those of Lord Rothschild and were kennelled at Ascott, near Leighton Buzzard. Most of the Williams family were keen on hunting.

The huntsman with his hounds in the grounds of Pendley Manor on the same day.

The Church Lads' Brigade form a guard of honour as the bride and groom leave Tring church after their wedding on 31 July 1907. The bride is Ivy Elizabeth Marion Williams, the daughter of the late Captain Stanley Williams of the 8th Hussars. Captain Stanley was Mr J.G. Williams' younger brother. The groom is Arthur Thomas Crawford Cree, the eldest son of Arthur W. Cree of Brockworth, Beckenham. The service was performed by the Revd E.D. Cree, the groom's great uncle and the Revd T.G. Cree, the groom's uncle, assisted by Tring's vicar, the Revd H. Francis. Below, the wedding reception at Pendley Manor. Today the manor is still frequently used for wedding receptions in the same beautiful setting enjoyed by this young couple more than ninety years ago.

A ram at the Hampshire Downs Sheep Sales on 20 July 1907, when Mr Williams put up sixty rams and seventy-five ewes for sale. That year he had considerable success in the Northampton and Peterborough agricultural shows and the sale attracted about two hundred breeders and others interested the sheep industry. The average price of the animals was £7 17s 6d, a very good price in those days. The expert shepherd, Mr H. Best, cared for the Pendley herd of Hampshire Downs sheep for many years.

Mr Frank Brown and Mr Donald Brown are here seen conducting the same sheep sale in the grounds of Pendley Manor.

Shire Filly "Ashwell Belladonna" 1st Prize Oxford Show 1910.
The property of J. G. Williams Esq. Pendley Manor, Tring.
Fed on Food Seasoned with Thorley's Food.

Mr J.G. Williams started farming in 1876 and after a modest beginning the Pendley Shire Stud became one of the most important in England. Year after year his horses won prizes at all the leading shows including the events put on by the Tring Agricultural Society of which Mr Williams was a member. There is still a Pendley Stud Farm and these days there are thoroughbred racehorses there.

Lincolnshire Red Shorthorn Heifer "Pendley Starlight 2nd"
The Property of J. G. Williams Esq. Pendley Manor, Tring
First Prize Royal Agricultural Show Gloucester 1909

Another speciality at Pendley Farm was the breeding of Lincolnshire Red cattle. This breed of beef cattle is nowadays uncommon except in the Lincolnshire area where it originated. It is a hardy and quickly maturing breed so it is more popular in Scotland. This heifer was one of the early champions to bear the prefix 'Pendley' in its name. The name is still carried on today as it is registered at Mrs Jennifer Williams' stud and all the horses and ponies bred there are registered with the 'Pendley' prefix.

47

A family group at Pendley Manor on 27 November 1910. Sitting in the centre is Mr Joseph Grout Williams with his wife, Catharine Mary, on his right. On his left is Mrs Ivy Cree, his niece, with her eldest daughter, Mary, while Mr Williams holds another daughter, Janet. Standing on the left is Mr Vivian Williams, Joseph's nephew, and on the other side Mr E.J. Nettlefold, who in the following year was to be best man at his friend's wedding to Miss Violet Wood. It is thought that the two younger men standing in the centre are also Joseph's nephews, he and his wife not having any children of their own.

The wedding of Mr Vivian Williams, the nephew and heir of Mr J.G. Williams, to Miss Violet Mary Thallussen Wood took place on 1 February 1911. The service was held at Aldbury church where Miss Wood's father was the rector and the reception was held at Pendley Manor. The two little attendants in the centre are Miss Mary Cree, the bride's niece, and Master Jackie Finch, the bride's cousin. The six bridesmaids are Miss Beryl Hawtrey, Miss Crawford and Miss Katie Finch, who were also cousins of the bride, and Miss Aline Tidswell, Miss Kenney and Miss Gillian Bloxam. The best man was Mr E.J. Nettlefold who, with the bridegroom, was in the 5th Dragoon Guards.

Pendley Manor is still renowned for its beautiful gardens. In the 1890s Henry Amos was head gardener to Mr J.G. Williams. By the first part of the twentieth century Frederick George Gerrish was in charge and by around 1920 it was Thomas W. Westcott, seen here with his staff. Back row: Charles Rance, ? Baker, Tom Reed, ? Cook, J. Gurney, ? Dell. Front row: ? King, Thomas W. Westcott, ? Kipper, Bill Harrop.

Joseph Grout Williams on his horse 'Danilo' in April 1920. When he died two years later, Pendley passed to his nephew, Vivian, who did not move to Tring as he had his home at Greens Norton, being master of the Grafton Hunt for some time. Joseph's widow, Catherine or 'Katy', still lived at Pendley outliving her husband by more than twenty years. Vivian's son, Dorian, returned to the house, which had been used by the Women's Land Army and others during the Second World War, and started to establish the Adult Education Centre there in 1945.

The funeral of Mr Joseph Grout Williams was on 13 October 1923. He had died on 9 October at the age of seventy-five. The Pendley farm was famous for the breeding of shire horses so it was fitting that two were chosen to pull the wagon carrying the coffin. They are seen above ready to leave the manor and below having just arrived at Aldbury church. The funeral service was conducted by the Rector of Aldbury, Canon Wood, and also by the Revd Claude Wood, from Croydon, Revd T.V. Garnier from Tring and Revd H.C. Finch from Wigginton. For those unable to go to Aldbury a memorial service was held at the same time in Tring Church where Mr Williams had been a churchwarden for more than forty years and Revd S. Mead officiated.

The first Mrs Vivian Williams was an accomplished horsewoman who rode side saddle with elegance. Here she is on her horse 'Cira' and the details with this photograph say that she had won first prize in the Ladies' Hack Class and first prize in the class for the officer's lightweight charger. Sadly she died in 1944 and some time later Mr Williams remarried. His second wife, Brenda, also shared his love of horses.

Mr Vivian Williams' second wife, Brenda, on her horse 'Little Model' performing the extended trot at a dressage event at Farnham Royal. Mrs Williams described herself as 'well past middle age' when she started dressage, but she trained her horses herself and was with the British Dressage team in two Olympic Games – Stockholm in 1956 and Rome in 1960.

Mr Dorian Williams, the son of Mr Vivian Williams, in the grounds at Pendley Manor with the script of Henry V. The Shakespeare Festival, which has continued to this day, grew out of the adult education classes that Dorian Williams started in 1945, at that time unique in this country. People of all ages could come to spend a few days in ideal surroundings to learn anything from pottery to horse management. The festival started with simple scenes from Shakespeare plays but by 1949 full performances attracted big audiences. Performed in the open air, the grounds provide an ideal setting and there have to date been very few occasions when bad weather spoiled the event.

The last of the Williams family to be at Pendley Manor, Dorian Williams and his wife, Jennifer. He described himself as 'brought up on horses and ponies' and was Master of the Whaddon Chase hunt from 1954 to 1980. He was also the best known commentator for the BBC at equestrian events, a role he took on in 1949. His wife, an equally enthusiastic horsewoman, specialized, as she still does, in the breeding and showing of ponies. This photograph was used on a Christmas card sent to family and friends.

Murray Fieldhouse is the tutor here at a pottery workshop held in the conservatory at Pendley Manor. Dorian Williams said of Murray: 'So obvious was his talent and his enthusiasm that a small pottery at Pendley seemed a worthwhile investment'. Thus one of the most popular classes in the adult education programme was introduced. Murray Fieldhouse is still a well known figure in the pottery world and has his studio near Aldbury.

The indoor riding school before it was altered to make the Pendley Theatre of today. It was originally built as an indoor tennis court and there are many records of parties and entertainments being held there. It was later used for riding but when this picture was taken it was only used for storage. It has now been transformed into a comfortable theatre and is used for the performances of plays and other events throughout the year.

A scene from *The Killing of Sister George* at the Pendley Court Theatre in April 1980. The play was directed by Robert Goldman and put on by the Actors' Repertory Theatre. June Fortune stars in the title role and with her are Heather Van Stratten as Mrs Mercy Croft and Harvine Higginson as 'Childie'.

The cast of a performance of *Arsenic and Old Lace* at the Pendley Court Theatre in 1982. It was put on by the Phoenix Theatre Company, successors to the Tring Theatre Company. The amiably nutty aunts, Abby and Martha, who specialized in poisoning people, are played by Barbara Kilpatrick and Zoë Young, their nephew, Mortimer, by Robert Mayson and his girlfriend, Elaine, by Teresa Edwards. This young couple are standing on the balcony and in the line in front are Harold Brown, Alan Bowling, Stephen Norris, Barbara Kilpatrick, John Copas, Zoë Young, Peter Cherry, Chris Ellis, Graham Lay, Val Warden and Bob Lawrie.

Husband and wife team, John and Jennie Branston, prepare for their entrances in *A Midsummer Night's Dream* in 1987. John as Theseus is riding 'Gulliver' and Jennie as Hippolyta is riding 'William'. The horses were supplied by the Gaddesden Place Riding School, well known for their services to riding for the disabled. When Dorian Williams was the director he made full use of the horses he had, to add authenticity to the plays. A fellow actor recalls of *Henry VIII*: 'Dorian played Wolsey but a troupe of seven horses received the greater applause!'.

Two programme covers from the Shakespeare Festivals. A large collection of these are displayed on the walls of Pendley Manor Hotel.

An atmospheric scene from a performance of *King Lear* in 1986. It shows actors John Branston as Kent, John Tolputt as The Fool and Jim Smith as King Lear. Dorian Williams recalling an earlier performance of this play said 'Perhaps the most remarkable of all Pendley's weather experiences was 1958 when, during a performance of *King Lear*, the storm of the century raged over North London. Three thousand flashes of lightning were registered; the thunder was incessant. But never a drop of rain fell on Pendley. It was, needless to say, startling and unforgettably effective.'

Pendley Beeches Lodge, one of several buildings designed by Tring architect William Huckvale to house members of Mr Williams' staff. An additional bedroom was built in upstairs in 1891, the carpenters being Messrs Grace and Jackson, who took two weeks to do the work, having signed the boards at the start and finish of the job. It was part of the Pendley Estate until 1971 when it was purchased by Frank and Barbara Reed as a family home. The footpath along the side of the lodge is now part of the Ridgeway Path and the building houses the Beechtrees Cattery and Kennels.

Four
Other Grand Houses

Perhaps Tring's grandest house is the Mansion, here *c.* 1975. It now houses the Arts Educational School.

Tring Mansion as it was before Lord Rothschild bought it in 1872. Thought to be designed by Sir Christopher Wren, it was built for Sir Henry Guy, groom of the bedchamber to King Charles II. After it was purchased by Baron Lionel de Rothschild the original formal appearance was completely altered, the conservatory removed and the house extended to look as it does today.

Wigginton Manor on the corner of Brook Street and Mortimer Hill was neither a manor house, nor was it in Wigginton. It was known locally by this name as Wigginton's legal affairs were dealt with here and reputedly there had been stocks in the road outside to punish evil doers from the village. As early as 1865, Joseph Marcham had a market garden here and later Mrs Marcham had a sweet shop at the side of the house. Edwin Smith had a builder's yard behind. A garage now stands on this area and, behind, a new road called Nursery Gardens.

Frogmore House in Frogmore Street housed the Butcher family in the nineteenth century and well into the next. Frederick Butcher was a well known Tring banker and his premises are now occupied by the NatWest Bank. By 1891 he was sixty-eight and had retired and lived in Frogmore House with his wife, Ann, and three unmarried daughters. The last owner, Mr Arthur Butcher, died in 1955 and the property was bought by the builders Janes and Company in June 1956. The house was then demolished and an estate of new houses was built, including Friars Walk and Deans Furlong.

The Furlong, a big house with its front on Park Road and the back, shown here, facing King Street. It was built by the Revd Pope, for some time vicar of Tring. In the 1930s it was occupied by Sir Gordon Nairne (1861-1945) who was a governor of the Bank of England and one of HM Lieutenants of the City of London. The Furlong was later used as part of the Convent School for girls but it has now been demolished and there is a recently built complex of dwellings on the site that bears the same name.

Home Farm, Park Road, was a fine house before the disastrous fire in the early hours of 5 February 1895. It was the home of Lord Rothschild's agent, Mr Richardson Carr, who fortunately woke and rescued his little daughter, Kitty, her governess Miss Fox, two female servants and a Mr Bathurst. Lord Rothschild's fire brigade arrived first, then the Tring brigade, but water pressure was low and they could not save the house. There were eighteen to twenty degrees of frost making conditions very difficult for the firemen; their saturated clothing was described as 'stiff as plate armour'. In spite of his own problems, Mr Carr sent down to the Rose and Crown for hot coffee and breakfast, supplied by Mr Jesse Thorne, for the tired workers.

The house and contents of Home Farm were insured by the Alliance office, of which Lord Rothschild was chairman. He arranged immediately to have the house rebuilt at an estimated cost of £4,000. Meanwhile he had a new wooden bungalow, seen here, built as a temporary home for Mr Richardson Carr. Towards the end of March that year there were severe gales. Several trees in Tring Park were blown down and the bungalow lost part of its roof. Home Farm is now called White Cloud House and the farm buildings have been converted to private homes.

Hawkwell in Station Road showing part of the beautiful big garden. In 1891 forty-seven-year-old Miss Eleanor Williams lived there with her sister, Harriet, also unmarried and seven years her junior. They must have been quite wealthy ladies as they also had six servants living in. There was a record of a Miss Williams in Hawkwell as late as 1937, perhaps the younger sister. Hawkwell stood in Station Road until the 1960s and part of the walled gardens were used for classes from Tring School. Hawkwell Drive now consists of twenty-five houses on the site of the house and grounds. The aerial view shows how extensive the grounds were.

This handsome house is Hollyfield in Grove Road. In the 1891 census it was the home of a thirty-nine-year-old Tring solicitor, Arthur W. Vaisey and his wife, Esther. They had two sons and six daughters, plus a governess and three servants who lived there. They would also have employed gardeners and other workers who lived in the town. Hollyfield survived until well into the next century when it was demolished to make way for the modern houses in Hollyfield Close.

Beech Grove in Station Road was the home of William Brown, the land agent, surveyor and valuer. He had the business that is now Brown and Merry in the same High Street premises. He died in 1890 at the age of seventy. His widow, Janie, continued to live there with her family, and their second son, Arthur McDonald Brown, carried on the business. Later in the next century the British Trust for Ornithology had the house for many years and when they moved to Norfolk it was left empty. This grand house, much larger than it appears in the photograph, has recently been demolished to make way for several houses to be built on the site.

The managers of the Silk Mill in Brook Street used to live in this substantial house with its lake and large garden. In 1881 the mill manager was thirty-three-year-old George R. Morton with his wife, Sarah. In the latter part of the century the occupants were John Akers and his wife, Elizabeth. The Silk Mill closed down but the Mill House has survived as a private home and in the first two decades of the twentieth century Walter Morris Thomas and his family lived there. Below they are seen in the garden, part of which was later taken to build some new houses, the road appropriately named Mill Gardens.

Drayton Manor on the Aylesbury side of Tring is one of the few grand houses that is still a private home. In 1891 Stewart W. Jenney, a seventy-four-year-old widower, lived there with his two sons, Stewart and Henry. There were also three servants, Elizabeth Batchelor from Aldbury, Sarah Fountain from Little Gaddesden and Tring-born Emily Brittain. Records of 1894 show that 'volunteer operations' were carried out in Drayton Park and the men were 'hospitably entertained by Captain Jenney'. In the 1940s and 1950s the house was a school for blind children, when twenty little boys and girls, their ages ranging from five to eight years, were taught and cared for there.

Stocks House, Aldbury, around 1905, showing the house before the extensive alterations that made it look as it does today. It seems to have been named after Richard Stokkis or Stokes, an earlier owner of the estate who sold it to William Duncombe in 1503. The house was built in 1773 by Arnold Duncombe, the last with the family name to own the estate, and there were considerable additions and alterations over the years. There were several owners and the well known Humphrey Wards were there from 1892 to 1920, but later it became Brondesbury school for girls.

STOCKS HOUSE, ALDBURY.

This more modern picture of Stocks House was probably taken in the 1950s when it was a girls' school. The photograph was made into a postcard sent out to invite people there on 14 July when the gardens would be opened from half past two to half past six in aid of the Aldbury District Nursing Association. Miss Doreen Harper would be giving a solo exhibition of juvenile cabaret dancing.

Nathaniel Rothschild purchased Champneys, near Wigginton, in 1902 from Canon Arthur Sutton Valpy, as a dower house for his wife, Emma, should she wish to leave Tring Park as her sons grew up and married. Nathaniel died in 1915 and later she sold Champneys and lived in the Tring Mansion for the rest of her life. After some time of private occupation, Champneys became Lief's Nature Cure Resort in 1925 and is still a popular health centre.

Aston Clinton House was the home of Sir Anthony Rothschild and his wife Louisa, whom he married in 1839. They bought the eighteenth-century house in 1853 and, considering it too small, added several new parts to the original building. Sir Anthony was financial adviser to Edward, Prince of Wales, who was a frequent visitor. During the First World War it became an army headquarters with training carried on in the parkland. After the war the house was shut for long periods and seldom used. Later it was used as a hotel but eventually the house was demolished and only the stable block remains today.

The manor and estate of Halton was purchased in 1853 by Lionel de Rothschild but the mansion was built by his son, Alfred, in the 1880s. Described as the 'free French château' style, this magnificent building has been preserved by the Air Ministry since they used it as an officers' mess at the end of the First World War. Lord Rothschild had offered the use of his estate at the beginning of the war and it was first occupied by the army.

Five
Farming

This medieval tile depicting farming is a copy of one of a set of eight tiles originally in Tring parish church and taken to the British Museum after the church was restored in the nineteenth century. Two other tiles went to the Victoria and Albert Museum. They illustrate Bible stories for the fourteenth-century congregation, most unable to read or write, and reproductions have just been commissioned by the Tring and District Local History and Museum Society. The story here tells of a master who chastised a workman for cutting a beam too short. Jesus came and pulled the beam to the right length and it could then be used as a plough.

The old Bunstrux barns on the Bunstrux manor, north of the town near where Frogmore Street becomes Dundale Road. Bunstrux House, said to date from the sixteenth century, was uninhabited for some time and was demolished around the middle of the twentieth century.

Tring farmer, Mr Chappell of Dunsley Farm, lost two valuable cows when they were struck by lightning in a thunderstorm on 19 June 1914. The local paper said that the photograph taken by Tring photographer, H. Humphrey, shows the exact position in which the animals fell, head to head, with the head of one resting on the other's forelegs.

Walter Mead's Highland cattle in the yard at Parsonage Bottom Farm. In the background is Western Road with the houses 'Elm House' and 'Westcroft' and the entrance to Langdon Street between them. Although most Highland cattle are now dun in colour, originally most of them were black. Here there is one of each colour and they must have been quite a novelty in Tring, as this hardy longhaired breed evolved to endure the harsh conditions in the Highlands and the islands around Scotland. This farm was on the site of what is now the Goldfield housing estate.

Parsonage Farm, here in 1956, was just behind Grace's barn in the centre of Tring. In 1851 the farmer was Joseph Gurney, employing eight labourers, by 1865 Peter Southernwood was there, towards the end of the nineteenth century there was James Darvill and at the beginning of the twentieth century Frank Grace, who also had a mill in Akeman Street. In the 1930s Alfred William Wright was followed by Arthur Lipscombe. Mr Lipscombe's daughter, Gwen, was well known in Tring, delivering milk from the farm, and later became Mrs Hummer when she married popular schoolteacher, Bob Hummer.

This picturesque wisteria-covered house is Grove Farm off Grove Road, near the Marshcroft Lane turn and not far from the big house, Hollyfield. It was the home of the Grange family for several generations. The 1891 census lists Herbert Grange, aged thirty, a corn merchant and farmer, with his wife, Ellen, three sons and a daughter. Mr Grange was the master of the Tring and District Farmers' Draghounds for some time. Sadly Ellen died in 1914 and two years later Herbert married Miss May Huckvale.

In the early days, haymaking required a very large number of workers. When scythes were used a line of men would move side by side across the field until all the grass was cut. The same process would be used for turning and raking up the hay as in this picture of Mr Williams' farm workers at Pendley.

The Pratt family of Great Farm, Marsworth, and their workers stop for refreshment during the harvest in around 1900. In order to make the most of good weather and daylight hours, work could not stop for long and food and drink was usually taken out to the fields during haymaking or harvesting.

Threshing was the traditional way of separating the corn from the ears. It was a long, tedious job but did provide work that could be done indoors in the winter months when harsh weather made it difficult to do other jobs outside. These days a combine harvester can do it all in a fraction of the time.

An early threshing machine is seen here at work on Pendley Farm. Although rather primitive, it could knock the grain from the ears and pass the straw through to be piled on the stack. It was worked by a steam traction engine.

Ted Delderfield, from the Marshcroft area of Tring, was said to be able to turn his hand to almost anything connected with hay, straw and ricks. In this picture taken in the late 1930s, he is operating a hay press. The twine at the base of the machine would be tied round when the bale was the right size. This is now done automatically by the modern hay baler.

Most of the farmers belonged to the Tring Association for the Prosecution of Felons. The Association was started in 1824 for the purpose of protecting the property of members and bringing to justice all felons offending against them. They produced posters offering rewards often many times the value of the animal stolen, presumably to encourage informers. In most cases chickens or a sheep would have been stolen to feed a hungry family. Records show that in 1845 a Mr George Webb was successfully convicted by solicitors G. & H. Faithfull and transported for life. By 1926, more than a century after it was founded, it was decided that the Association was no longer needed as conditions had changed over the years and so a year later it was wound up and the assets divided among local charities.

Lamb Stealing.

15 Guineas

REWARD!

STOLEN on Saturday Night last, or early on Sunday Morning, a FAT LAMB from a Field called " White Hawkwell," in the Occupation of Mr. BENJAMIN CROUCH, of the Parsonage Farm. Tring :—

WHOEVER will give such Information of the Offender or Offenders as shall lead to his or their Conviction shall receive from the

Tring Association

a Reward of

TEN GUINEAS,

and from Mr. BENJAMIN CROUCH a further Reward of

FIVE GUINEAS;

and an Accomplice impeaching the other shall be entitled to the like Reward.

Apply to Mr. J. R. GLENISTER,

Treasurer and Secretary to the said Association.

TRING, HERTS.
April 29th, 1833.

BUTTFIELD, PRINTER, &c. HEMEL HEMPSTED.

Sheep Stealing.

TEN GUINEAS

REWARD!

WHEREAS on the Night of Monday last, or early the following Morning, some Person or Persons entered a Sheep-fold, in a Field called 'Windmill Pen,' at MISWELL FARM, and slaughtered a Wether Sheep, belonging to Mr. BENJAMIN CROUCH, leaving the Head, Skin, and Entrails, in an adjoining Field, and the Carcase in the Icknield Road.

Whoever will give such information, as shall lead to a Conviction of the Offender or Offenders, (whether an Accomplice or otherwise,) shall receive the above Reward on application to

Mr. GLENISTER,

Treasurer to the Tring Association.

TRING, 7th June, 1837.

[PATTISSON, PRINTER, TRING & BERKHAMSTEAD.

The dairy at Lord Rothschild's Home Farm in Park Road. Designed by William Huckvale in red brick and tiles, it stood in its own garden. The main hall was floored in grey and white marble with a fountain in the centre. Blue tiles covered the walls and there were marble slabs on which stood containers for the milk and cream, and butter-making utensils. Miss Cole, in charge in the 1890s, would carve flowers and other fancy shapes from the butter. The Rothschilds' milking herds were Jersey cows and a cart loaded with churns of milk would go to Tring Station twice a day and the milk would be sent up to London. The dairy is now a private house.

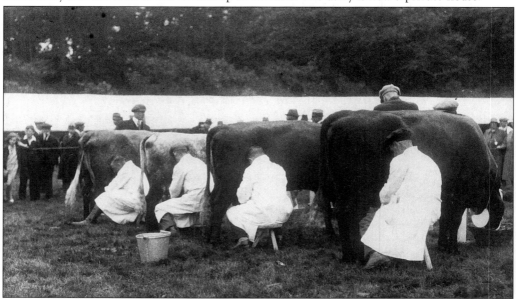

Cows being milked at Tring Agricultural Show. A milking competition and butter tests were introduced to the show by Lord Rothschild in 1893, who the following year is recorded as having given £200 in prizes. A well fitted marquee was supplied for churning and making up the butter and the standard was very high, over a quarter of the entries yielding over 2 lbs of butter from one day's milking.

Horses being led down the High Street to Tring Show around 1900. Many competitors in the show, which was the largest one-day event in the country, came a considerable distance and the horses would have been stabled overnight locally to arrive at the show ground early the next morning. The building just behind the leaders was the surgery of Dr James Brown and Dr Edward Pope. Beyond that was Joseph E. Lawson, grocer and tea merchant, and on the Akeman Street corner was George Jeffery the chemist.

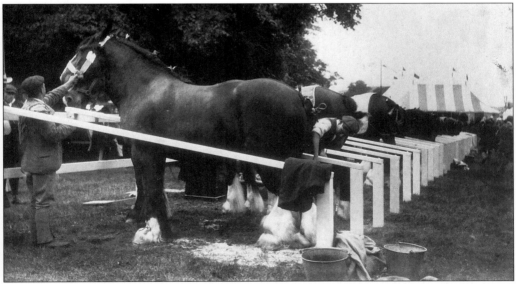

Shire horses being prepared for their entry into the ring at Tring Show. Lord Rothschild, 'Natty', had the most successful shire horse stud of all time. His stud manager, Tom Fowler, was reputed to have been able to spot a future champion almost from the time it was born, and he undoubtedly improved the shire horse as a breed in Britain. It was said that Natty would never exhibit his own horses at Tring, feeling that, with his stables full of champions, it would be unfair to visiting competitors.

A busy scene at Tring Show in 1904. There is no doubt that the popular show did much to improve the quality of livestock in the area as a high standard was required to win the prizes on offer. The Tring Agricultural Show continued until just before the Second World War and after it the Herts County Show was held in Tring Park for a number of years.

A very early picture of the cattle market in Brook Street with a sale of pigs in progress. Wigginton Manor can be seen in the background. This fine building was later demolished to make way for the Market Garage.

76

Six
At Work

This picture is by Tring photographer Arthur John Norman, who had his studio in Western Road towards the end of the nineteenth century and the beginning of the next. It was taken in Mr Grace's workshop, possibly in Frogmore Street. The present Mr Gilbert Grace still has the large flywheel and iron gates shown in this photograph. Back row: Sam Budd, ? Gower (father of Oliver), Charles Grace, Walter Rance, ? Austin. Front row: ? Pitkin, Fred Grace (son of Charles), ? Ives.

Alfred Minall, Lord Rothschild's taxidermist, in his workshop. When still a child, Walter Rothschild was inspired by Alfred's interest in wildlife and his collection of animals and decided to have a museum of his own. His first 'museum' was in a shed at the end of a garden in Albert Street with Alfred as its guardian and taxidermist. For his twenty-first birthday Walter's father built him a museum and, at Walter's request, a cottage to house the Minall family. These were designed by Mr William Huckvale and built by Tring builders J. Honour and Sons.

Mr W. J. Rodwell poses with a group of young ladies and boys in 1917. They were preparing baskets to take shells for use in the war and are in the yard of the Royal Hotel at Tring Station.

The canal system was started towards the end of the eighteenth century and was used as a route for barges carrying freight until well into the twentieth century. It was essential that the waterways were kept clear and in the picture above Peter Mew is in the 'Bulbourne Weedcutter', fitted with machinery for clearing the water weed. In the photograph below, this long team of heavy horses is pulling an ice-breaking craft. If the winter was very hard a prolonged frost could mean real hardship for the barge families. A report in the winter of 1895 stated that seventy-five canal boats were icebound and could not get from Fenny Stratford to Tring and that their 350 occupants were 'in a very destitute condition'.

The Silk Mill in Brook Street. The mill was built early in the nineteenth century and at its busiest was employing nearly five hundred people, including children as young as seven years old. The employers, Evans and Co., started to lose money when silk goods were imported from the Far East in direct competition. The business was taken over by Lord Rothschild who ran it at a loss while reducing the labour force until it was closed down. He removed the top three floors and replaced the roof, to make it the long low building it is today. It became the estate timber yard and workshop and was later taken over by the Royal Mint and after that the RMR Engineering Works.

Young lady workers in the assembly rooms at the RMR pose for a photograph outside the factory before starting work in the summer of 1957. Back row: June Welling, Dawn Wright, V. Penn, Sally Eggleton, Iris Meager, Megan Oakley. Front row: Dorothy Poulton, Dorothy Barber, Marjorie Spencer.

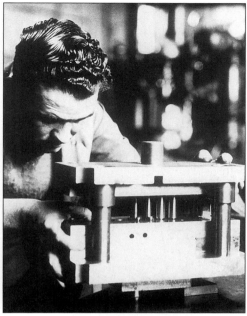

At Christmas 1889 Lord Rothschild presented 300 silk mill workers with a new silver crown. He also gave a tea party at the Victoria Hall for the workers and their families and personally handed out gifts to them. One of the recipients was James Teddar who had worked at the mill for fifty-eight years. Here, nearly a century later, we have two of the skilled workers employed by the RMR: Mr George Anderson, a tool turner, and Mr Bert Disbury, a toolmaker.

When the Second World War started, the RMR works adapted to help the war effort and made detonators and small parts for aeroplanes. In peacetime they made lipstick cases among other things. Pictured here is another product, the bus conductors' ticket machine. The old silk mill now consists of several units housing small businesses.

Workmen building new reservoirs at Tring. It is thought that this must be at Dancers End as the main Tring reservoirs were built very early in the nineteenth century, well before photography was invented. The original print was a postcard, not used until later in the century. The reservoir must have been in use by 1895, as during the fire at Home Farm, referred to elsewhere, Dancers End was contacted to try to increase the water pressure for the firemen's hoses, unfortunately without success.

Mr Frank Prentice's Chiltern Bus Company in around 1933, at their Western Road garage. From left to right: Frank Prentice, Sid Harris, Albert Saunders, -?- , ? Bly, -?- , Tom Cook (mechanic), ? Butler, Perce Eeley, -?- , -?- , -?- , Les Boiling, ? Bachelor, Fred Flitney, -?- , ? Saunders, -?- , Ted Brocklehurst.

82

The Tring Museum in Akeman Street employs a large number of mainly local people. Here is part of the workforce that was there in 1982. Back row: Arthur Kitchener, Bob Pilkington, Maurice Bradding, Cliff Ellis, Eunice Watkin, Ron Routley, Eileen Williams, Olive Major, Michael Walters, Vera McKernan, 'Mac' McKernan. Middle rows: 'Jock' Brown, 'Effie' Warr, Tim Wood, Arthur Wood, Pam Landau, Peter Dawson, Vic Mayhew, Helen France, Sarah Ferri. Front row: Ian Galbraith, David Snow, Anne Vale, Graham Cowles, Dave Horah, Peter Colston, Jo Bailey, Derek Read.

Sheep being sold in the cattle market in Brook Street by auctioneer Mr Stephen Hearn. The market used to be held in the High Street, then called Market Street. The Rothschilds provided a purpose-built market in Brook Street in the 1880s. Animals are no longer sold but Mr Hearn now has his auction business there with general sales twice a month and a regular fine art sale with paintings, furniture, silver, porcelain etc.

Tring volunteer firemen tackling a blaze over the shop at No. 10 Akeman Street in the 1960s. Dudley Fulks at the top of the ladder directs the hose through the window. Mrs Haywood used to sell fascinating objects in the antique shop, which is now the pet food shop run by Hazel Lockton. At the tuck shop Mary Menell sold snacks and sandwiches and in the background Arthur Sayer had his barber's and hairdressing business.

Seven

Schooldays

Tring Junior School in around 1950. Built in 1842, the Tring National School housed, at that time, about 100 boys and some 70 girls, who were taught by a master and a mistress with the help of monitors. The building was enlarged in 1866 and again in 1874 to make more classrooms for the ever increasing number of pupils. Records show that classes could contain as many as ninety pupils of mixed abilities, often in rooms barely capable of housing such numbers. It was demolished in 1982 and the new library and car park now occupy the site. The drinking fountain just seen on the wall to the left has now been mounted on the wall by the entrance to the Memorial Garden.

This photograph, although in very poor condition, has been included as it is a unique picture of Miss Bess Allen's girls' class at Tring School, around 1920, before the introduction of mixed classes. Back row: ? Jacock, Kath Lovegrove, Betty Rodwell, -?-, ? Horn, Olive Allibone, Daphne Nutkins, Wynne Hearn. Middle row: Mavis Baker, Cissie Bly, ? Rawlins, Jane Cowen, Doris Gower (in white hat), Vida Kitchen (in black hat), -?-, -?-, -?-, Frances Hearn (in beret), ? Kitchen. Second row: ? Horn (part hidden), Grace Harrop, Joan Gibb (with hair bow), Kitty Attryde (with blonde bob), Mary Gillingham, -?-, Connie Brackley (in dark skirt), Edna Rogers (with her hand over her eyes), Molly Batchelor. Front row: -?-, -?-, Ivy Poulton, Queenie Boiling, Evelyn Clarke.

A class of Tring School around 1922 with their teacher Miss Madge Waterton. Back row: Miss Waterton, Harold Kindell, -?-, Harry Cutler?, -?-. Third row: -?-, -?-, -?-, -?-, Cissie Randle, Kath Westcott?, -?-, -?-. Second row: Edie Edwards, Alice Crockett, Gladys Hart, Elizabeth Collier, -?-, -?-, Stella Burton, Lena Ives, Fred Hoare (kneeling). Front row: Maurice Boniface, Freddie Keen, -?-, Percy Dwight, -?-, Fred Goodson, Fred Oakley, Wally Wilkins.

Tring School Standard Seven in 1930. Back row: Maurice Boniface, Fred Goodson, Arthur Cartwright, Arthur Higby, Harold Wells, Harry Cutler, Wally Crockett, Alf Pearce, Bill Edwin, Ted Neale. Middle row: Percy Dwight, Wally Rance, Gerald Coe, Warren Griffin, Ken Luck, Jack Bridges, Bert Lawrence, Ted Marsh, Rowland Stevens, Alfie Hearn, Cyril Mansfield. Front row: George Rance, Fred Philby, Tom Hedges, George Christopher, Fred Brady, Eric Nutkins, Ron Desborough, Laurie Watts, Gus Proctor.

Class of Tring School in 1948 with teachers Miss Bukoke and Miss Baker. Back row: Elizabeth George, Maureen Simpson, John Linton, Dennis Capel, Kathleen Stone, Marjorie Spencer, Christopher Matthews, Norman Jelley, Gillian Newton, Pat Kirk. Middle row: Christine Whittington, David (Podge) Price, Jean Bannister, -?-, David Richardson, Martin Kempster, Mary Rowe, Doreen Catlin, Leslie Horne, Stephanie Wilkins. Front row: Pamela Johnson, Mabel Fowler, Ronnie Ives, Brian Britten, Pat Bracket, Brenda Poulton, Malcolm Hewitt, Edna Finney, Colin Lovegrove.

A Tring School group around 1950 with teachers Mr Thomas and Mr Gibbons. Back row: -?-, -?-, Norman Howe, Joe McAllister, Melvin Collier, -?-, -?-, Edward Golightly, Cecil Evans. Third row: Owen Christopher, -?-, Jean Collier, Marion Bryant, -?-, Judith Simmonds, Phyllis Tofield, Neville Kempster, Alan Frazier. Second row: Sheila Clark, Jill Bateman, Joan Blandon, Dorothy Archer, Marna Byde, Valerie ?, Brenda Jeffery, -?-, -?-. Front row: John Springett, David Higby, John Keen, Godfrey Halsey or Brian Impey, John Rance, Tommy Keen.

Tring School class of 1951 with teachers Miss Bacon and Mr Varty. Back row: Tony Higgs, John Weedon, Desmond Gurney, Margaret Nash, Joan Smith, Judy Bligh, Maureen Flynn, Norman Howe?, David Burnett. Third row: Marion James, Ann Wright, Elsie Jeffery, Irene Brackley, Vanda Badrick, Sheila Bavin, Christine Eggleton, Yvonne Sharp, Joy Wainwright, Anne Bateman. Second row: -?-, Eileen Rogers, Margaret Bell, Ann West, Brenda Drake, Rosemary Hilliard, Mary Eeley, Lily Keogh, Rosie Mead, Doreen Butler. Front row: Henry Batchelor, Gerald Lond, Michael Colby, Joe Hitchman, Patrick Ward.

Tring School class in the mid 1950s with teacher Mr Miller (The Duke). Back row: Len Cousens, -?-, David Harvey, -?-, Trevor Ellis, John Fountain, -?-, Jimmy Golightly, -?-, -?-. Third row: Mr Miller, -?-, Barry Skingle, -?-, -?-, -?-, Lily Poulton, -?-, John James, Raymond Puddifoot. Second row: -?-, Margaret Doyle, Vera List, -?-, Dorothy Pearsell, Sandra Harris, -?-, Renee Wills. Front row: Eric Higby, -?-, Robin Bryant, Horace Bond, David Gunn, ? Webb.

Tring School class of 1956 with teacher Mrs Reed. Back row: Tony Bishop, Tony Ackroyd, Jonathan Hearn, Michael Dale?, Reed Fryer, Alan Carter, Reggie Moorcroft, Rodney Puddifoot, Nigel Bide. Middle row: John Hart, June Hinton, Wendy Brinklow, Paula Carter, Linda Moss, Yvonne Yoro, Maureen Prior, Ena Gregory, Trevor McAllister, Stewart Nutkins. Front row: Ann Simmons, Doreen Organ, Barbara Hearn, Muriel Downs, Janet Revell, Rosemary Cockman, Judy Price, Wendy Dawson, Diane Stevens.

A Tring School group around 1957. The teacher on the right is Miss Baker. Back row: Susan Sayer, Martin Bagnell, -?-, Terence Pope, Michael Bannister, Robert Hall, Richard Clark, Michael Wagstaff, Terence Gower, Michael Goodman, Rosemary Prentice. Third row: Barbara Richardson, Heather Putman, Penelope Southgate, Margaret Kempson, Susan Batchelor (?), Evelyn Tippett, -?-, Geraldine Gordon, Glenda Jackson. Second row: -?-, -?-, Maureen Swanson, Jennifer Organ, Rosemary Wood, Pamela Clough, -?-, Coral Johnson, Diane Organ, Janet Lovell. Front row: John Smith, Stephen Smith, -?-, John Slocombe, Richard Cook, David Purbrick, David Smith, Brian Horton.

Musical winners at Tring School in 1963. Back row: Alison Woodward, Vicki Marshall, Gillian Young, Dawn ? , Beverley Adams. Middle row: Colin Ralph, John Wagstaff, Linda Whicker, -?-, Jane ?, Michael Kempson, -?-, Jill Bousted, Stephen Burrows. Front row: Janet Clough, Alison Holder (?), Christine Pearsall, Miss Baker, Mr Hamilton, -?-, Mrs Kaye, Eileen Eastham, Virginia Meakin, Susan Wright.

A Tring School class in the 1960s with teacher Mr Hart. Back row: Michael Eggleton, Kevin Gomm, Maurice Amer, David Bull, Michael Hartley, Peter Routley. Third row: Philip Mitchell, Tony Webb, Graham Miles, Glynn Poulton, Graham Hawes, Robert Stevens, Jean Wheeler. Second row: Heather Powell, Gail Cartwright, Janet Young, Carol Goodman, Linda Eggleton, Rachel Dineen. Front row: Valerie Hill, Susan Gomm, Christine Wright, Elizabeth Molson, Linda Chapman, Pat Butler, Charmaine Leggett, Hazel Clough.

The teachers at Tring School in the 1960s. Back row: Miss Bishop?, Mr Blake, Bill Riddaway, Mr Woodward, Mr Bracher, Mr Jennings, Mr Edney, Mr Hart. Front row: Mrs Thomas, Miss Caroll, Miss Simmonds, Bill Green, Mr Thomas, Mrs Hewitt, Miss Speed, Miss Auger, -?-.

A class of Tring School with teachers Mr Thomas and Mr Les Tarmer. Back row: Ken Wainwright, Gregory ?, George Brooks, -?-, David Kempster, John Couchman. Third row: Margaret Stone, Eileen Blackburn, June Drake, Pat Dwight, Jean Flitney, Audrey Cooper, Eileen Kempster, Jean Webb, Daphne Green. Second row: Shirley Price, Kathy Nutkins, Rita Burch, -?-, Jean Parslow, Margaret Ropert, Margaret Keogh, Maureen Dufour, Maureen Bradding. Front row: -?-, -?-, Dudley Fulks, -?-, -?-.

In the first half of the twentieth century there were several private schools in some of the larger houses. Here at Elm House, on the corner of Western Road and Langdon Street, records show that in 1917 there was a girls' school run by the Misses Daisy, Frances and Lily Collins. Before this it had been the private residence of Mr Edward Joseph Le Quesne MB, who was a surgeon and medical officer for Tring and district. It was, however, occupied very much earlier, as in 1841 William Griffin, aged ninety, lived here with Mary Ann Griffin nearly fifty years his junior. Langdon Street was known as 'Griffin's Lane' for many years. In 1851 Mary Ann, then described as a widow, was still there, living with her niece, twenty-three-year-old Sarah Elliman. Elm House looks much the same today and is at present used for commercial purposes.

Eight
Free Time

The Church Lads' Brigade in Tring, *c.*1909. The Brigade was founded by Walter Mallock Gee in 1891 and the first company was opened at St. Andrew's Church, Fulham. The object of the Brigade was to extend the Kingdom of Christ among the lads and to encourage faithful membership of the Church of England. The methods used by the early Brigade were built on military discipline and obedience. In 1911 the War Office recognized the Church Lads' Brigade as cadets and later they adopted the khaki service dress uniform. The military uniform and drill of the brigade, originally adopted for purely symbolic reasons, were given greater meaning with the onset of the First World War when the Church Lads' Brigade members formed two battalions of the King's Royal Rifle Corps and gained many war honours. Although they are not doing so here, in several photographs of Tring Church Lads' Brigade the boys are carrying rifles. Here the chaplain was the Revd H. France, and the officers were Captain Revd D. F. Slemeck, Second Lieutenant C. P. Cole, warrant officers H. Randall, S. G. Tite, F. C. Rance, G. T. Ross, F. E. Rance and W. Rance.

The Church Lads' Brigade Football Club, *c.* 1911. Back row: E. Cross, A. Bradding, H. Budd, L. Bull, A. Crockett. Middle row: R. Grace, R. Wright, T. Smith. Front row: F. Rance, W. Smith, F. Parker, C. Butcher, W. Cartwright.

During the time that the Rothschilds occupied Tring Mansion, they opened the park to the public on several occasions, the best known being the Agricultural Show held each year in August. This photograph from the early 1900s shows a carousel set up in Tring Park for the amusement of local people.

Tring Town Football Club outside the cricket pavilion, c.1905. Back row: -?-, -?-, -?-, -?-, F. Rance. Front row: Arthur Baldwin?, Arthur Hedges, Jesse Dewey, Vic? Bull, Faddo Waring, R. Wright?.

The Ladies' Meeting of the High Street Baptist Chapel around 1910. On the back row of four Mrs Lucy Impey is on the left at the end and Mrs Emily Brackley at the opposite end. The two ladies standing at the right end of the next row are Mrs Ellen Kingham and Mrs Pearce. Mrs Kingham was the wife of Mr Benjamin Kingham who founded his cycle shop in Western Road in 1904. She lived to be 101, Tring's oldest lady, and the first centenarian since the beginning of the century when Mr James Stevens died at the age of 103. Mrs Pearce was the wife of the Revd Charles Pearce who was the minister at the chapel from 1874 to 1920, so long that its was known locally as 'Pearce's Chapel'. Sitting in front of Mrs Kingham is Mrs Ann Impey. In the small group at the front with the children, Mrs Ginger is on the left and Mrs Noah on the right.

A Tring ladies' group, *c.* 1915. Back row: -?-, Mrs Minall, Mrs Elliman, -?-, -?-. Middle row: Mrs Randall, -?- (baby), -?- (baby), -?-, Mrs Collier, Laura Rance, -?-, -?- (baby), -?-, -?-. Front row: -?-, Mrs Nash, Jessie Hearn, -?-, Annie Collier, -?-.

Tring's successful tug-of-war team pose with their trophy. Back row: Sid Bradding, ? Rowe, David Lovegrove, George Barber, Fred Gray. Front row: Fred Hearn, Albert Clarkson, Sam Marshall, Jack Tugby, ? West.

Skating on the Wilstone Reservoir, thought to be about 1920. For several years in the 1890s the papers reported that the reservoirs were in a safe condition for skating, so there must have been some severe winters. The thickness of the ice would be checked to ensure safety and on one occasion a Mr Gordon Thomas set twenty men on clearing the snow for the skaters. These days it is rare to find the reservoirs frozen hard enough for skating.

The Tring YMCA gymnastics team, *c.* 1914. They are outside the YMCA headquarters in Tabernacle Yard in Akeman Street. The yard still has the same name but the old tabernacle has been demolished and replaced by modern houses.

New Mill Cricket Club team, 'married v. singles', in the 1930s. The match was played at Grove Park, now built over and called Bunyan Close. Standing: Bert Healey, David Ashwell, Arthur Nutkins, Arthur Marchant, -?-, ? Blake, ? Wilkins, Arthur Underwood, Tom Edwards, Gus Proctor, Percy Healey, Jack Boarder, ? Smith, -?-, ? Gower, Len Dean. Sitting: Ernie Kindell, Eric Birch, Bill Drake, Jack Rance, A. Putman, 'Shuffy' Horn.

A photograph taken at the Tring British Legion's first annual fête in 1932. It was held in Tring Park and the Mansion can be seen in the background behind the maypole dancers. As early as 1914 the maypole with children dancing round was pictured in front of the mansion, when May Day celebrations were organized by Mrs Minall, the wife of Lord Rothschild's taxidermist.

The Wigginton Brass Band in 1927. Back row: R. Seabrook, A. Langston, Fred Copcutt, G. Butchers, L. Bignall. Third row: B. Herridge, H. Dell, Reg Hearn, Rob Hearn, Arthur John Copcutt. Second row: P. Dell, G. Dell, S. Beasley, J. Dell, -?-, F. Dell. Front row: F. Dell (standing with drum), H. Gurney, -?-, George Bradding, A. Lines (bandmaster), Revd Drake, J. Reason (honorary secretary), E. Lampkin, C. Hearn, H. Rowe (standing with drum).

A group of members of the High Street United Free Church with their shield for gaining the highest score in the West Herts section of the National Scripture exam. In the centre of this picture, taken in the 1930s, is Mrs Ellen Kingham, who trained scholars for the exam until she was seventy years old and was a member of the United Free Church until she was 100. Back row: Mr Hulsden, Mr J. Brooks, Jack Kingham. Middle row: -?-, -?-, -?-, Cyril Knapp, Mrs Ellen Kingham, Cyril Ginger, -?-, Roy Emery, Reg Brooks. Front row: ? Metcalfe, Olive Emery, Dulcie Stevens.

Members of Tring YMCA celebrate Christmas with a sausage and mash supper in the mid 1930s. Back row: Walt Batchelor, Frank Bly, Bill Edwin, Lionel Cyphus, Stan Wright, Tom Fulks, Fred Waterton, Frank Johnson. Next row: -?-, Phil Keen, Tom Paget, Alf Hearn, Rudolf Consterdine, -?-, Frank Rogers, ? Wright, Jim Harrop, Sid Rance. Group of four on left: Fred Horn, Gilly Rance, Bert Wright, Ernie Childs. Four on far side of table: Ted Bagnell, Doug Westcott, Harold Brackley, Peter Bowley. Front row: Roland Rance, Gus Proctor, Arthur Edwards, Roy Waterton, Eric Nutkins, Harold Wells.

A tableau, 'Britannia and her Daughters', at the end of a glee party concert given in the Victoria Hall by the Women's Section of the British Legion on 4 January 1938. Britannia was Mrs Buckingham, England Mrs Lovell, Scotland Mrs Rance, Ireland Mrs Ives, Wales Mrs Cooper and Peace Mrs Budd. The concert was first performed on 29 December and it was repeated the next week to raise funds for the children's party. Members of the men's branch worked hard behind the scenes, including Mr W. Cartwright who provided the decorative backgrounds and Mr George Sayer who conducted the Legion Band.

The New Mill Follies, a local entertainment group, put on a revue in the 1940s. They are Barbara Hunt, Phyllis Gates, -?-, Jean Illing, -?-, Doris Baldwin, 'Bill' Smith, Pam Saunders, Audrey Mansfield, 'Tucker' Smith and, sitting, Daphne Hummerston.

The First Tring Scout Group at their camp at 'Leylands', St Leonards, August 1948. Back row: ? Connell, David Copcutt, Robin Bussell, Donald Erridge, Les Batchelor, Ted Wright, Peter Cook, ? Dole, George Tite, Ralph Wood, John Turner, John Copcutt, Don Theobald. Middle row: Philip Gibbs, Jack Kingham, Pat Deverell. Front row: Philip Prentice, Bill Hawtin, ? Brooks, George Turner, Tony Saunders, Alec Rance, Jimmy Rance, John Howlett, Lionel Hitchings.

New Mill Youth Club meets to celebrate the New Year in 1946-47. Front table, clockwise from the left-hand corner: Avis Burch, Jeff Poulton, -?-, Ernie Edwards, Muriel Stratford, John Butler, Josie Russell, Audrey Dover, Richard Lyons, Barbara Brackley, Rosie Eggleton, Richard Stratford, Joan Verney, -?-, Shirley Snow, Kathy Hearn, -?-, Billy Sharp, Carol Prior, -?-, J. Wright, Mr Mills. Back table, clockwise from the far side: Derek Kempster, Jill Bandy, Ron Rance, -?-, -?-, Muriel Goddard, -?-, Betty Gunn, Bernard Evans, Alice Putman, ? Lewis, Muriel Barber, Bobby Hart. Group in the centre: Dusty Miller, Sylvia Burch, Stella Burch, Joe Jakeman, Clifford Keen, Winnie Eggleton. Standing: Mr Wren, Mr Rance, -?-, Ralph Seymour, Mrs Dover, Mrs Brackley, ? Smith, Teddy Kempster; the rest are unknown.

Tring Red Cross. Back row: Joe Ridley, Mrs Yates, Dina Reeves, Molly Percival, Rosemary Keen, Jean Kitchener, Joan Allen, Erica Guy. Middle row: Beryl Perkins, Mary Watson, Mary Chapman, Ruby Boniface, Gladys Hull, -?-, Shirley Blake, -?-. Front row: Janet Ford, Joan Cole, Joan Watts, Vera Hare, Nora Grace, Dr Thallon, Margo Baines, Betty Wood, Mrs Mary Whittaker.

Bank holiday coach outings were organized by Mr and Mrs George Walker for more than twenty-five years. Here they are visiting Wannock Chase. Back row: Jim Meager, Mrs Meager, Mr Crouch (driver), Jack Caterer, Mr Budd, Mrs Budd, Bert Archer, Clifford Kesley, Mr Eustace. Third row: -?-, -?-, Miss Fanny Hobbs, Miss Mary Hobbs, -?-, -?-, Mrs Rance, Mrs Eustace, Miss Violet Kesley. Group of three in centre: Mr George Walker, Mrs Higgs, Mrs Kath Walker. Second row, standing: Mrs Simmonds, Mr Bob Wooding, Mr Budd, Mrs Budd, Mr Baldwin, Mrs Baldwin, Mr George Rance, Mrs Florrie Rance, Mrs Turner, Mr Turner, Mrs Darville. Front row, sitting: Mrs Whittle, Mrs Nellie Wooding, Mrs Nora Smith, -?-, Joe Walker, Mrs Walker, Mrs Brooks, Mr Brooks.

The Akeman Street Baptist chapel choir giving a concert in the church schoolroom in 1957. Back row: Bob Church, Albert Higby, Mr Bradding, Mrs Bagnall, Miss Burch, -?-, Dawn Wright, Marjorie Spencer, John Smith, Bert Prentice, Pastor Pibworth. Middle row: Alfie Wright, Ken Rance, Margaret Digweed, Audrey Bateman, Nelly Brandon, Miss Rance, Mrs Lawrence, ? Foster, -?-. Front row: Jean Sayer, Hilda Wright, Joyce Hoare, Dorothy Dix, Connie Wright, Margaret Bass.

Tring Fire Brigade and their families having a Christmas party around 1960. Back row: Mrs W. Rance, Doris Baldwin, Dennis Bradding, Noreen Bradding, John Foskett, Wally Rance, Florence Saunders and Dudley Fulks. The next row starts with Charlie Cummings, in uniform cap. The next couple with the baby are unknown, then Ivy Bradding, Doug Sinclair, Peg Foskett, Mrs L. Hooper, and Mary Gosling. At the end of the row are Bill Giddings and Tom Saunders. Among the children are: Doug Sinclair Jnr, Malcolm Carlisle, Chris Gosling, ? Gosling, Malcolm Bradding, Patsy Carlisle, Gail Sinclair, Graham Foskett, Alan Foskett, Mavis Sinclair and Brenda and Patricia Robinson.

The Vale Gilbert and Sullivan Society seen here performing, not in one of their popular light operas, but in a cabaret put on at one of their dances in around 1978. From left to right: Rosemary Southworth, Paul Bridle, John Rotheroe, Richard Cook, Stewart Collins, Jenny Waller, Kate Collins, John Castle.

Nine
Special Days

The Conservative Club in the High Street decorated for Queen Victoria's Diamond Jubilee in 1897. The event was celebrated in June that year and it was decided to put a commemorative window in the parish church. The window, the work of Mr E.C. Kempe, was unveiled before Evensong on Easter Monday in 1899. In 1898 preparation had started towards building the New Market House on the Akeman Street corner of the High Street, as another memorial to Her Majesty's Jubilee, to be built by public subscription.

A group of cyclists from Tring gather on Ivinghoe Beacon for a picnic on 26 April 1897. A Tring Bicycle Club started in 1896 with their headquarters at the Rose and Crown. From April to August they arranged runs every Wednesday afternoon and Saturday evening. Outings that year included runs to Windsor on Easter Monday and later trips as far as Watford, Luton and St Albans.

The people of Tring gather to hear the chairman of the Urban District Council, Mr Frederick Butcher, read the proclamation of the accession of King Edward VII on 4 February 1901. In front of the platform in the New Market House stands a guard of honour formed by the F Company of Volunteers commanded by Major William Stewart Jenney. Shortly before, the major and some of his men had formed part of the guard at Windsor for the funeral of Queen Victoria. On the platform with Mr Butcher are Tring's vicar, Revd S. Tidswell, Mr J.G. Williams of Pendley Manor and Mr A.W. Vaisey, clerk of the Urban District Council. The church bells rang to celebrate the day, unmuffled for the first time since the Queen's death.

The Tring Church Lads' Brigade and Church Girls' Brigade march down the High Street, then still called Western Road, around 1905. They would parade through the town when there was a religious festival to celebrate. On the left it can be seen that the police station has yet to be built.

In 1905, horses still provided the main means of transport. Here, on 21 July of that year, the Pendley Mothers' Meeting is setting off for an outing. The lamp on the side was essential as it was illegal to have a carriage on the road after dark without one. A few years earlier a gentleman named Lavender Seabrook was seen by PC Knight driving in Tring without a light on his cart and was brought before Berkhamsted Petty Sessions where he was fined 12s 6d.

Tring celebrates the coronation of King George V on 23 June 1911, with flags across the road and people thronging the High Street. The shops kept a selection of Union Jacks, some of which exist to this day, to welcome royalty to the town, particularly the King's father, Edward VII, who visited Lord Rothschild at Tring Park on several occasions.

This postcard was posted on 8 June 1914. It shows the Church Sunday School treat on Whit Tuesday with John Collins and Frank Minall carrying the banner, being followed by the Tring Band. They all went up to Tring Park where the correspondent states: 'We had it fine for the children until about 6.30 when a steady drizzle sent us all out of the park'.

The people of Tring gather for a National Day to celebrate the peace after the First World War, on 19 July 1919, the treaty having been signed on 28 June. The soldiers who had returned requested that the day should begin with a short informal service in front of the war memorial to honour those who gave their lives. The Revd Henry Francis conducted the service and also two more in the parish church to celebrate the National Day of Rejoicing. The memorial was unveiled on 27 November the previous year and there were 105 names carved on it.

On Armistice night, November 11 1937, Mr Wilson, the manager of the Gaiety Cinema in Akeman Street, invited the British Legion to have a remembrance festival in the cinema. A Legion film *Men of Yesterday* was shown and the vicar of Tring, Revd C. T. Wood, conducted a short service. Standard bearers held the flags of the Tring, Wigginton and Aldbury branches of the Legion. Later a shower of poppy petals fell from the roof. To accompany the choir and the community singing the British Legion Band provided the music. Among the bandsmen on the left are Stan Rance, A. Miller, ? Copcutt and 'Pimp' Rance. In the centre is the conductor, George Sayer, and the group on the right includes Fred Copcutt, Jim Impey, F. Mills, ? Wright, G. Doodey and George Bradding.

Tring people eagerly joined in the parades for the Silver Jubilee of King George V and Queen Mary on 6 May 1935, the biggest celebration since the end of the First World War in 1918. Here Robert Hedges, with parasol, stands by his float outside his fruiterer's and general shop, just after you turn into Miswell Lane. With him is his brother in law, Harry Bone, who took over a general store further up the same road in 1957. Harry's shop continued, run by his son, Mervyn, until his retirement in 1997.

On their way to Tring Park for the Silver Jubilee celebrations in 1935 is the YMCA horse-drawn float passing the George Hotel in the High Street. All are dressed in eastern costumes and standing by the palm tree is Frank Bly. Sitting at the base of the tree is 'Nobby' Rance.

A little later the same day the floats have arrived in Tring Park to join the crowds already there. Tring Mansion can be seen in the background.

Tring YMCA with their Widdicombe Fair group celebrate the Coronation of King George VI and Queen Elizabeth on 12 May 1937. They made the grey mare from a vaulting horse from the gym club. Back row: Roy Waterton, Gus Proctor, Alf Hearn, George Rance, Peter Bowley. Middle row: Stan Wright, Fred Waterton, Len Lovegrove, Arthur Waldock, Tom Paget, Charlie Kempster (by horse), Cyril Delderfield, Bert Wright (above sign), Frank Johnson, Eric Nutkins. Front row: Ralph Allen, Roland Rance, 'Noddy' Rance (holding sign).

A celebration dinner is being held here to welcome Tring servicemen home after the Second World War. Among those here are: First table, left-hand side: Mr Saunders, Norman Jeffery, Ted Cutler, Mr Horne, Ray Eggleton. Right-hand side: -?-, Mr Minall, Mr Welling, Mr Wright. Second table, left-hand side: Bert Brooks, Tom Keen, Jesse Wilson, Jim Eely, Mr Heley. Right-hand side: Mr Doody, John Barber, Mr Collinge, Mr J. Veal, Mr Edwards, May Edwards, F. Barter. Third table, left-hand side: Sonny Keen, Mr Connell, Mr Thame, Mr Rogers. Right-hand side: Percy Dwight, Bill Messenger, ? Butler, Jack Oliver, Eddie Russell, Mr Routley. Standing at the back: -?-, Tom Tyler, Mrs Philby, Mr Dando, Mr Christopher, -?-, 'Splash' Kempster, Mr Baldwin, Mr Barber, Mrs Welling, Mrs A. Kempster, Mrs Rogers.

Tring celebrated the Coronation of Queen Elizabeth II on 2 June 1953. Bob Hedges had spent most of the previous day creating this magnificent display of hydrangeas and other flowering plants. Here he is standing in front of his Miswell Lane shop with his wife, Ruby, and his mother, Ada. The shop is still a busy general store and is now called 'The Old Stables'.

Ten
Transport

Miss Jessie Grace was the first woman to have a bicycle in Tring. Here she poses at Grace's mill in Akeman Street, now known as Grace's Maltings. She is on a tandem tricycle with her brother Frank in the early 1890s.

Cyclists gather outside Pendley Manor for a day's outing on 15 April 1898. The bicycle was invented in 1839 but it was not until the 1880s, when the cycles were lighter and more comfortable, that they became universally popular. Cycling clubs sprang up all over the country and it became acceptable for ladies to wear their skirts a little shorter to make it easier to ride their bicycles, although modern women would not dream of trying to cycle in the costumes worn by these ladies.

Two lady cyclists by the stocks in Aldbury with the church and pump house in the background, c. 1902. It is clear that bicycles were especially made for ladies to accommodate the voluminous skirts that they were still expected to wear.

Even after the introduction of the motor car it would be more usual to see horse-drawn vehicles in Tring until well into the twentieth century. Here Archie Gower is delivering merchandise from J. Gower and Sons in the Lower High Street. They covered a fairly large area; here they are outside cottages at Dagnell.

Later Gower's acquired a motor van for their deliveries. Here Archie's brothers, Nathaniel and Benjamin, stand by a very early model.

Young Tom Grace sits in his father's Jackson Sports Model car, *c.* 1912. Frank Grace, who owned the Maltings in Akeman Street, was one of the first people in Tring to have a car. Tom and his brother, Bob, grew up to be well known as local historians and their 'Old Tring' lantern lectures have been enjoyed for many years.

This Riley Tri-car of 1904 is being ridden by Gilbert Charles Grace with his son Gilbert Harold Grace in front. G. Grace and Son started servicing cars in the workshops in Parsonage Place at the beginning of the century, and today specialize in the care of classic cars. The connection with Riley Cars is still maintained, since Mr Gilbert Grace is a Vice President of the Riley Motor Club.

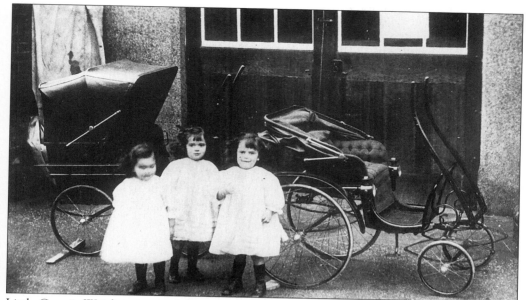

Little Connie Wright poses with her sisters, twins Madge and Muriel, in front of a pair of baby carriages. On the continent these could have been pulled by big dogs. Draught dogs were banned in England in 1854 so a Shetland pony would have been the ideal choice, though old photographs show older brothers or sisters in the shafts.

This 1910 10½-litre Fiat racing car is being driven by Frank Lockhart, well known in Tring for his coal merchant's business in Western Road. In the 1950s he raced at Silverstone and Oulton. The car itself was raced at Brooklands, lapped at 115 mph, and was driven by John Cobb, racing driver and land speed record holder.

New Mill supporters of Luton Football Club stop for refreshment at The Travellers' Rest in the mid 1920s. By the car are: Alf Pilgrim, Bill Akers (looking out of the window), 'Tink' Turney, driver unknown, -?-, Charlie Holliman.

The showroom at Wright & Wright's garage in Western Road in 1929. The firm was established in 1870 by Mr George Parrott as coach builders and wheelwrights. Later he took as his partner Mr A.S. Wright, who had been his apprentice. Mr Parrott retired in 1910 and his half of the business was sold to Mr Wright's cousin, Mr Robert Wright. It was then called Wright & Wright. The boy in the centre is fourteen-year-old Frank Ware who worked for the firm until he died in the late 1980s, never having missed a day's work through illness.

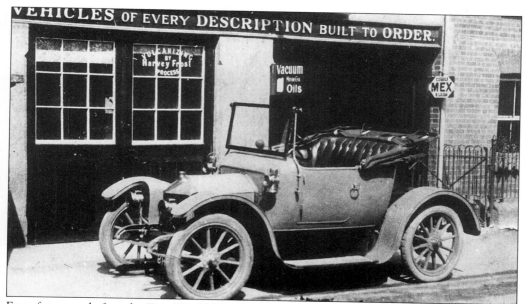

For a few years before the First World War Wright & Wright built cars like this one mainly on a Mors chassis. About thirty workers were employed to build these by hand and the firm exhibited at the 1913 motor show at Olympia. In the First World War their workshops produced small trucks for the War Office and in the early twenties they were dealers for Ford, Austin, Rover, Morris and Wolseley cars.

The first Aylesbury-Watford-London bus was built at Wright & Wright's and the roof had to be raised on the workshop entrance to get it out when it was finished! This aerial photograph taken in the 1950s shows the premises considerably enlarged but more recently the square house and some of the workshops have been demolished to provide more forecourt parking space. Today the garage specializes in Hyundai cars, although they keep a wide range of other makes and models.

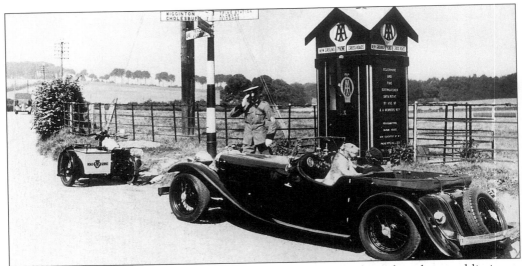

The Automobile Association was founded on 29 June 1905. In those days the speed limit was 20 mph and the AA were said to give priority to warning their members if they were approaching police speed traps. At first their smartly dressed patrolmen rode bicycles but later used their familiar motor cycle and sidecar outfit. By 1950 the AA had a million members and more than nine million drivers are members today, although we can no longer expect the courteous salute as we drive by. This AA box stood at New Ground where the back road to Aldbury turns off the Tring to Berkhamsted road, then the A 41.

One of the earliest records of the motor car in Tring was when one passed through the town in November 1898, causing a considerable amount of interest. Once the car became popular it was necessary for petrol to be available for sale. This early petrol pump was by Vine Cottage, a house that stood where the entrance to the telephone exchange is now and the little lane alongside was known as Pleasant Row. Mr Stan Cook ran his garage for many years in this area. Bull's general store can just be seen on the right.

The Gem Cinema in Western Road only survived until the early 1920s, due to competition from the Gaiety Cinema in Akeman Street. Here, later in the same decade, it is being gutted to form part of the garage for Mr Ebenezer Prentice's Chiltern Bus Company. The site was later used by the Unigate Dairy and now houses the Post Office sorting office.

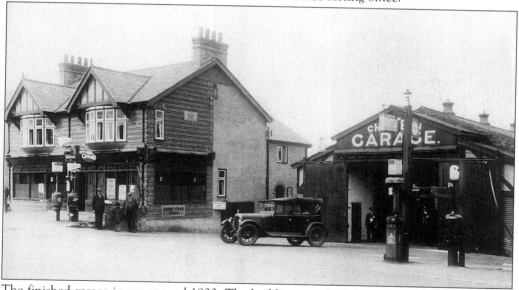

The finished garage in use around 1933. The buildings on the left were purpose-built in 1928 as a private office and a booking office. They are now a pet shop and a video shop, though many people will remember the nearest one as Magees, also a pet and animal foodstuffs shop for many years. The group standing by the entrance are Mr Frank Prentice, the son of the founder of the Chiltern Bus Company, his daughter, Mary, and his brother-in-law, Mr Ted Brocklehurst. In 1933 the business was taken over by the London Passenger Transport Board.

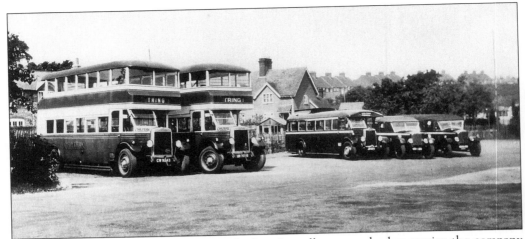

Some of the Chiltern Bus Company's vehicles. As well as a regular bus service the company offered pleasure trips with coaches and charabancs. The Rothschild houses in Goldfield Road can be seen in the background and beyond them the houses in Miswell Lane.

Transport in Western Road in 1939. The design of the double-decker bus has altered little in over half a century. There are plenty of cars here but soon most of them would be off the road as the petrol ration for private use was discontinued during the war. The procession, led by the Salvation Army band, consists of volunteers ready to help the war effort and they have just passed the top of Christchurch Road.

Eleven
Nearby Places

This photograph was taken in March 1886 and is a very early picture of Aldbury village, showing the thatched cottages that were later demolished. They were Mr John Grover's bakery and barn and are on the site of the present village stores, post office and Memorial Hall. An even earlier photograph exists that shows the Church House across the road from the barn. It was in very poor condition and had been knocked down before this picture was taken.

Aldbury in August 1920. The three little girls posing by the pond are Janet, Eleanor and Mary Cree. Although this view has not changed, the deserted road would seem strange to villagers these days. The open space is usually crowded with cars belonging to visitors to the Greyhound, one of the most popular public houses in the district.

THE CANAL · WILSTONE ·

The Grand Union canal at Wilstone. Built towards the end of the eighteenth century, when it was called the Grand Junction canal, it went from Braunceston to London. Work started in June 1793 and it cost about a million pounds to build. The costs rose because of inflation caused by the Napoleonic wars. Around six thousand workers were required as all work was done by hand. As natural springs alone did not supply enough water to feed the fifteen locks in this area, the first reservoir was built at Wilstone in 1802.

Puttenham in the early 1920s. The village, now much smaller than it had been in earlier centuries, was named after the de Puttenham family descended from a Norman follower of William the Conqueror. The Manor of Puttenham was described in the Domesday Book of 1086 as being owned by the Bishop of Bayeux and occupied by Earl Leofwine. It consisted of a manor house, cottages, meadows for ploughing and pastures for livestock.

Wigginton Bottom or Lower Wigginton, a hamlet to the south of Wigginton. The Lamb public house can be seen in the distance. In the 1891 census the beerhouse was run by thirty-five-year-old George Rowe, his wife Annie Elizabeth and their four children. Next door was a general shop run by Mr and Mrs Kingham. Life was hard in early times, especially in days of drought, until mains water came to Wigginton around 1870. Oil lamps were the main means of lighting until electricity came to the village around 1928.

Standing on Long Marston crossroads early in the twentieth century. In 1865 the village was described as a hamlet and chapelry to Tring, $3\frac{3}{4}$ miles to the north of the town, partly in Buckinghamshire and partly in Hertfordshire. The population at the time was around 440 and the priest was the Revd Henry Auber Harvey MA who preached alternately here and at Wilstone. There was a railway, the line coming from Aylesbury, but no station; passengers were picked up and set down at Long Marston Gates. William Kay was the chief landowner and lord of the manor.

Long Marston in the 1920s with the National School on the right. In 1900 the headmistress was Miss Hannah Pamment who lived in the school house with her mother and sister. The buildings were destroyed by bombs during the Second World War. On the left is the Boot public house. In the 1891 census fifty-six-year-old William Roberts, his wife Elizabeth and their five children were living there. The Boot was also hit by the bombs that destroyed the school and tragically there was a fatality in this incident. The pub was later rebuilt and is still thriving and supplies a good range of food and drink.

Pitstone Green Post Office.
Nr Tring.

Photo, Copyright,
H. Humphreys, Tring.

Pitstone around 1905. Ancient names of the village were Pittleston and Pincelstorne and it was described in the Domesday Book as belonging to the Earl of Morton. The late sixteenth-century manor came into the possession of the Cheyne family and later descended to the Dukes of Bridgwater who also owned Ashridge. The local Pitstone Green Farm Museum is popular for visitors during the summer months when extra attractions include tractor rides, old working engines and craft demonstrations.

The Canal, Marsworth

The canal at Marsworth, c. 1915. The thatched cottage by the towpath was then a beer house and probably a small general store supplying provisions to the families on the passing barges. It was later a general shop and in a book recommending walks in the area, published in 1986, it was described as a café. There is the Marsworth reservoir nearby, one of four built in the area to feed the canal network.

The White Lion at Startops End, Marsworth, c. 1905. Henry Chapman was the publican. The Grand Union canal runs alongside the public house; the gentleman on the right is leaning against the bridge, and one of many locks on the canal is just beyond the other side of the bridge. Opposite the cottages is another one of the four Tring reservoirs, also named Startops End.

Lord Rothschild offered his Halton Estate for the use of the Services before the First World War when it was used extensively for training purposes. The Air Ministry took over in 1918 with the house and grounds being partly refurbished by German prisoners of war. This postcard, dated 12 September 1929, was sent by young apprentice aircraftsman Alder to let a friend know that he had passed his medical exam, been given his uniform and started drill. He also says that there were three to four thousand boys there at that time. Just over a decade later many of them were no doubt defending their country in the Battle of Britain.